Co-Teaching
& Collaboration

A Collection of Articles

From *TEACHING Exceptional Children*

Barbara Ludlow
Editor

Council for Exceptional Children
The voice and vision of special education

ISBN 0-86586-471-3

Contents

Acknowledgment

The Council for Exceptional Children would like to extend a special thank you to Barbara Ludlow for her continuing contribution to the field. It is under her leadership as editor of *TEACHING Exceptional Children* that these articles were selected and published in this collection.

Introduction

Barbara Ludlow

Some might say that collaboration is rapidly becoming a fundamental value in today's world. Thomas Friedman, Pulitzer Prize winning columnist for the *New York Times*, set the tone for the new century when he proclaimed that the world is now flat (Friedman, 2005). He suggests that this flattening is due in large part to emerging digital technologies that have opened new opportunities for worldwide social interactions and global economic structures. He argues that these tools have created an unprecedented need for collaboration in business, government, and education

The Partnership for 21st Century Skills, an alliance of key education associations, nonprofit organizations, and commercial businesses, has identified collaboration as one of the core skills for learning and innovation needed by all learners in the 21st century (Partnership for 21st Century Skills, n.d.). Effective schools must help students learn to collaborate so they can be successful in mastering knowledge and skills in the digital age and in preparing themselves to be competitive for the jobs of the future. To support students in integrating knowledge and skills across the curriculum, teachers must themselves engage in collaboration as they plan units and lessons, select instructional strategies, design learning activities, and assess student progress and outcomes.

Collaboration is also a cornerstone of current best practices in the discipline of special education. The Council for Exceptional Children has identified collaboration as one of the key professional content standards for the preparation of all special education teachers (Council for Exceptional

Children, 2009). The importance of collaboration in professional work is documented by its inclusion in the standards for initial preparation of beginning teachers as well as the standards for advanced preparation of specialists. This recognizes the fact that the complex needs of each exceptional child cannot be met by one individual but instead demand the best efforts of professionals from a wide array of disciplines as well as family and community members and other support personnel.

Special education can never be a solitary endeavor. To effectively and efficiently promote development, learning, and achievement by students with exceptionalities, whether they have high-incidence or low-incidence disabilities or are gifted and talented students, special educators must coordinate their efforts with a host of other people who support that child. As a result, the need to collaborate permeates every aspect of the special educator's role, from initial assessment and decision making to determination of eligibility for services, development of the individualized education program, delivery of instruction in the context of the standards-based curriculum, monitoring of learner progress, and assessment of learning outcomes. But perhaps no component of collaboration is more critical than co-teaching.

EVOLUTION OF COLLABORATION IN SPECIAL EDUCATION

Collaboration has been a fundamental component of special education ever since the right to education was established for students with special needs. In 1975, the United States Congress mandated a free, appropriate public education for all students with disabilities and required that assessment, planning, and program delivery be accomplished by multidisciplinary teams in partnership with parents to meet each child's individual needs (Joiner & Sabatino, 1980). Around the same time, other countries began to pass similar laws that granted access to public education to students with disabilities. These developments stimulated a rapid expansion of special education services within the broader context of general education in the public schools.

In 1986, Madeleine Will, then Assistant Secretary of Education, proposed that general education and special education be merged into a single service system, known as the Regular Education Initiative (Jenkins, Pious, & Jewell, 1990). As more students with disabilities began to be served in general education classrooms, there was a greater need for special educators to coordinate their work with that of elementary and secondary educators. Over the next decade, these activities and relationships evolved from less to more involvement (consultation to collaboration), and from indirect to direct engagement (participation in meetings to co-planning and co-teaching).

When the Individuals with Disabilities Education Act (IDEA) was reauthorized in 1997, schools were required to provide all students with disabilities access to the general education curriculum (Wolfe & Harriott, 1998). This intensified the need for collaboration between special educators and general educators in the determination of eligibility for services, in the development of individualized programs, in the selection of placements, and in the integration of instructional activities in the classroom using a variety of co-teaching models.

The reauthorization of the Elementary and Secondary Education Act in 2001, popularly known as No Child Left Behind (NCLB) required schools to assume responsibility for educational outcomes for all students, including those with special needs (Simpson, LaCava, & Graner, 2004). By mandating that all students be taught by teachers highly qualified in their content areas, this law made it necessary for general educators with training in academic content methods to collaborate with special educators with training in specialized instructional strategies to deliver appropriate educational programs to students with disabilities through co-planning and co-teaching activities.

Shortly after, the 2004 changes to IDEA reinforced the mandates of NCLB and required schools to initiate early intervening services using a responsiveness to intervention model to prevent academic failure of struggling students (Fuchs & Fuchs, 2006). This law further increased the need for general education teachers and special education teachers to work together to support all students in achieving proficiency in the state's standards-based curriculum. Today, co-teaching has become the heart of collaboration in special education as special educators and general educators coordinate their efforts to design and deliver individualized instruction that addresses both academic content standards for the grade level of every student as well as personal learning goals identified on the individualized education program for students identified with disabilities.

Co-teaching and collaboration are now firmly established as core values and practices in education. Initial research suggests that classrooms and schools in which collaboration occurs are more likely to produce better student performance and outcomes (Cook & Friend, 2010; Gruenert, 2005). Changes are taking place in many schools to promote collaboration through activities such as co-teaching by general and special educators, co-planning in educational teams by content area or grade level, and co-therapy through embedding related services specialists in classrooms. Changes also are taking place in teacher education programs to support collaboration in the schools by requiring general and special educators to take courses in collaboration (Arthaud, Aram, Breck, Doelling, & Bushrow, 2007), designing collaborative teacher education programs (Pugach, Blanton, & Correa, 2011), and requiring dual certification in general and special education for all teachers (Blanton, Pugach, & Florian, 2011). These developments clearly show that the discussion in today's schools, colleges, and universities no longer centers on whether co-teaching and collaboration are needed but rather on how to make them work.

OVERVIEW OF CO-TEACHING AND COLLABORATION

Co-teaching and collaboration depend on two key elements: (1) practices that allow individuals to coordinate their actions toward a common goal, and (2) values that allow individuals to respect and nurture their work together. These elements operate in a bidirectional dynamic—while fostering collaborative cultures leads to more collaborative activities (Seashore Lewis & Wahlstrom, 2011), it is also true that putting in place collaborative structures leads to more collaborative cultures (Pugach, Johnson, Drame, & Williamson, 2012). How each partner approaches the co-teaching relationship is affected both by beliefs and by practices.

Some research shows that collaboration is affected by differences in teachers' beliefs about the learning abilities of students with disabilities and in the extent to which it is appropriate to modify the curriculum to address individual needs (Carter, Prater, Jackson, & Marchant, 2009). A review of the literature on the interaction between evidence-based practices and teacher collaboration also revealed that the instructional strategies favored by general educators and those favored by special educators reflected very different assumptions about how learning occurs (Van Garderen, Scheuermann, Jackson, & Hampton, 2009). These findings suggest that such philosophical and practical differences may be barriers to successful collaboration and to achieving student learning outcomes unless educators are willing and able to negotiate such differences and interweave multiple strategies to support individual students.

Despite (or perhaps because of) the centrality of collaboration to special education, practicing effective co-teaching, co-planning, and co-assessment does not always come easy. Collaboration takes time—time to develop supportive working relationships and time to plan and conduct coordinated activities. Yet, teachers often report that they face challenges in finding enough quality time to engage in collaborative activities (Leonard & Leonard, 2003). Collaboration also may require additional effort. A recent study of new teachers (Youngs, Jones, & Low, 2011) found that novice special educators faced more demanding curriculum and role expectations and needed to develop collaborative relationships with a wider variety and greater number of individuals than their general education colleagues.

So, what does it take to make co-teaching and collaboration work? Marlene Pugach and her colleagues (2012) identify five qualities of successful collaborative professionals: (1) they recognize that complex goals require coordinated action, (2) they are willing to share responsibility and recognition; (3) they have faith that the group can solve problems, (4) they see working together as an opportunity for personal growth, and (5) they reflect on the outcomes of their own practice. If students with exceptionalities are to have equal access to and equitable outcomes from a free, appropriate public education, it is essential that teacher educators cultivate these qualities in prospective teachers, that school administrators provide training and resources to support their development in practicing teachers, and that general education teachers and special education teachers themselves nurture their growth throughout their careers.

STRATEGIES FOR MORE EFFECTIVE CO-TEACHING AND COLLABORATION

This collection of articles from past issues of *TEACHING Exceptional Children* offers ideas for fostering effective and efficient co-teaching and collaboration in today's schools throughout the multiple activities associated with co-teaching. The book opens with some thoughts on how to create, nurture, and sustain truly collaborative relationships between general education and special education teachers. In "Co-teaching: Getting to Know Your Partner, " Jane Sileo uses the metaphor of a marriage to describe the co-teaching relationship as a framework for effective practices in collaboration. The author discusses how to build the relationship through planning processes and to grow and maintain the relationship through problem-solving strategies.

Wendy Murawski and Lisa Dieker state that co-teaching, like any marriage of two different people, requires time and effort, and they offer tips for helping that marriage survive and thrive in "50 Ways to Keep Your Co-Teacher: Strategies for Before, During, and After Co-Teaching." Their ideas cover a wide range of activities that all teachers can use to promote collaborative values and implement collaborative practices before, during, and after co-teaching to promote satisfying relationships and achieve desired results.

All too often general educators and special educators focus on co-planning and co-teaching efforts, forgetting that these activities also require co-assessment to be successful. In "Purposeful Assessment Practices for Co-Teachers," Greg Conderman and Laura Hedin focus on assessment in the context of co-teaching, an activity that requires the most sophisticated collaboration between teachers. The authors offer suggestions for how general educators and special educators can work together to select and conduct assessments before instruction to plan lessons, during instruction to monitor student learning, and after instruction to measure progress.

In this era of school accountability for education of all students, it is vital that general educators and special educators work together to assess student progress to meet targeted learning outcomes. In "Teachers Working Together: Improving Learning Outcomes in the Inclusive Classroom—Practical Strategies and Examples," Amy Lingo, Sally Barton-Arwood, and Kristine Jolivette describe specific activities each teacher can engage in to coordinate assessment activities in the context of the most commonly used assessment procedures: anecdotal records and notes, student work samples and other products, event recording, and formal data recording.

The most effective collaborative efforts may be pointless if they are not based on the use of evidence-based practices for teaching content. So, in "Creating Optimal Opportunities to Learn Mathematics: Blending Co-Teaching

Structures With Research-Based Practices," Jane Sileo and Delinda van Garderen describe how to incorporate research-based instruction in mathematics into each of six different co-teaching structures, discuss challenges that blending the two may present, and offer strategies and resources for integrating them in everyday practice.

Successful collaboration requires skill in adjusting activities planning, teaching, and assessment in the contexts of specific schools and classrooms. Because secondary school settings pose unique challenges for co-teaching, Nancy Rice, Elizabeth Drame, Laura Owens, and Elise Frattura asked teachers and other school personnel to talk about what skills they thought were necessary for successful co-teaching. In "Co-Instructing at the Secondary Level: Strategies for Success," the authors offer a series of case studies that illustrate how co-teaching pairs conceptualize and practice six skill clusters across content areas and grade levels.

Meaningful collaboration takes time, and teachers often argue that they do not have enough time for planning, let alone for coordinating their planning activities. Because time for teachers to plan together is often limited, Wendy Murawksi offers ideas for maximizing the outcomes of co-planning time and a sample co-planning format in "10 Tips for Using Co-Planning Time More Efficiently." She describes how to find a time and place conducive to joint planning, focus efforts on planning processes during the meeting, allocate each teacher's time during the lesson to support the student most effectively, and prepare a co-planned lesson plan for later use.

Because collaboration requires bridging the gap between different assumptions about learning, individual teaching styles, and personal communication and interaction skills, collaboration is not always as easy as it sounds. In "Don't Give Up! Practical Strategies for Challenging Collaborations," Sharon Cramer and Jan Stivers share a series of vignettes that show common problems teachers encounter when interacting with colleagues. The authors offer strategies for developing one's own collaboration skills through developing a personal resource network, participating in other professional communities in the school, and collecting data to track progress in improving the problematic collaborative relationship.

It is not enough to practice collaboration and hope for the best—educators must also reflect upon and measure the success of collaborative efforts. Recognizing the centrality of good working relationships to effective collaboration, Kathryn Wiggins and Sharon Damore offer a 6-component model of collaboration in "'Survivors' or 'Friends'? A Framework for Assessing Effective Collaboration." The authors explain the six elements of positive attitude, team process, professional development, leadership, resources, and benefits, and then describe a process for evaluating a school's collaborative efforts using a rubric, a checklist, and an action plan.

Finally, collaboration occurs not just between two teachers in a classroom; it also occurs across multiple individuals who support educational programs for students with and without special needs. In the closing article, Elise

Frattura and Colleen Capper propose a new model of organizing school teams to support inclusion of all students with disabilities in general education classrooms in "New Teacher Teams to Support Integrated Comprehensive Services." Their integrated approach to inclusion describes how four teams should coordinate efforts to support individual students: the school planning team, the school service delivery team, the grade-level design teams, and the district-wide service delivery team.

These 10 articles represent some of the most recent practical applications published in *TEACHING Exceptional Children* on the many elements of successful co-teaching and collaboration. The articles are assembled to provide an overview of some of the best suggestions offered to readers of the journal over the last several years. Please enjoy these ideas for how to make collaboration work from the very people who strive to make it work every day in their own schools and classrooms.

REFERENCES

Arthaud, T. J., Aram, R. J., Breck, S. E., Doelling, S. E., & Bushrow, K. M. (2007). Developing collaboration skills in pre-service teachers: A partnership between general and special education. *Teacher Education and Special Education, 30*(10), 1–12.

Blanton, L. P., Pugach, M. C., & Florian, L. (2011, May). *Preparing general education teachers to improve outcomes for students with disabilities.* Washington, DC: American Association of Colleges of Teacher Education. Retrieved from http://ldaofmichigan.wikispaces.com/file/view/AACTE+NCLD+Policy+Brief+May+2011sm.pdf

Carter, N., Prater, M. A., Jackson, A., & Marchant, M. (2009). Educators' perceptions of collaborative planning processes for students with disabilities. *Preventing School Failure, 54*(1), 60–70.

Cook, L., & Friend, M. (2010). The state of the art of collaboration on behalf of students with disabilities. *Journal of Educational and Psychological Consultation, 20,* 1–8.

Council for Exceptional Children. (2009). *What every special educator must know: Ethics, standards, and guidelines* (6th ed.). Arlington, VA: Author.

Friedman, T. L. (2005). *The world is flat: A brief history of the 21st century.* New York, NY: Farrar, Straus & Giroux.

Fuchs, L. S., & Fuchs, D. (2006). A framework for building capacity for responsiveness to intervention. *School Psychology Review, 35*(4), 621–626.

Gruenert, S. (2005). Correlations of collaborative school cultures and student achievement. *NASSP Bulletin 89*(645), 43–55.

Jenkins, J. R., Pious, C. G., & Jewell, M. (1990). Special education and the regular education initiative: Basic assumptions. *Exceptional Children, 56*(6), 479–491.

Joiner, L. M., & Sabatino, D. A. (1981). A policy study of P. L. 94-142. *Exceptional Children, 48*(1), 24–33.

Leonard, L. & Leonard, P. (2003, September 17). The continuing trouble with collaboration: Teachers talk. *Current Issues in Education* [On-line], *6*(15). Retrieved from http://cie.asu.edu/volume6/number15

Partnership for 21st Century Skills (n.d.). *Learning for the 21st century: A report and mile guide for 21st century skills*. Washington, DC: Author. Retrieved from http://www.p21.org/storage/images/stories/otherdocs/p21up_Report.pdf

Pugach, M. C., Blanton, L. P., & Correa, V. I. (2011). A historical perspective on the role of collaboration in teacher education reform: Making good on the promise of teaching all students. *Teacher Education and Special Education, 34(3)*, 183–200.

Pugach, M. C., Johnson, L. J., Drame, E. R., & Williamson, P. (2012). *Collaborative practitioners, collaborative schools* (3rd ed.). Denver, CO. Love Publishing Company.

Seashore Lewis, K., & Wahlstrom, K. (2011). Principals as cultural leaders. *Phi Delta Kappan, 92(5)*, 52–56.

Simpson, R. L., LaCava, P.G., & Graner, P. S. (2004). The No Child Left Behind Act: Challenges and Implications for educators. *Intervention in School and Clinic, 40(2)*, 67–75.

Van Garderen, D., Scheuermann, A., Jackson, C., & Hampton, D. (2009). Supporting the collaboration of special educators and general educators to teach students who struggle with mathematics: An overview of the research. *Psychology in the Schools, 46(1)*, 56–77.

Wolfe, P. S., & Harriott, W. A. (1998). The reauthorization of the Individuals with Disabilities Education Act (IDEA): What educators and parents should know. *Focus on Autism and Other Developmental Disabilities, 13(2)*, 88–93.

Youngs, P., Jones, N., & Low, M. (2011). How beginning special and general education elementary teachers negotiate role expectations and access professional resources. *Teachers College Record, 113(7)*, 1506–1540.

Co-Teaching: Getting to Know Your Partner

Jane M. Sileo

Mr. Salvatore and Ms. Happa were getting to know one another. They were in a new co-teaching partnership, designed by the school administrator, since just before the school year began. Mr. Salvatore had been a solo fourth-grade teacher for 15 years. He enjoyed teaching and maintaining complete instructional responsibility for students in his classes.

Ms. Happa was new to the school. She had been a teacher for 7 years and enjoyed collegial interactions on behalf of students for whom she and other teachers shared responsibility.

In the beginning of their teaching arrangement, Ms. Happa was comfortable in a supportive role because she wanted to learn about the students and Mr. Salvatore's teaching style. As time passed, however, she wanted a more active instructional role and increased opportunities to interact with students, especially in the upcoming implementation of response to intervention (RTI).

Co-teaching is analogous to a professional marriage (Scruggs, Mastropieri, & McDuffie, 2007) in which teaching partners collaborate to provide instructional services to students with disabilities and others at risk of school failure as a result of the negative consequences of environmental events. Regrettably, in many instances co-teachers are carelessly placed together and therefore, completely miss out on the development stages critical in a relationship. As in conventional marriage, skipping the time to develop a strong relationship may lead to communication problems and misunderstandings, as well as ending the relationship. These difficulties between adults can negatively affect

students in co-teaching settings. For example, students may receive conflicting messages when there is friction in a co-teaching relationship and the teachers are not synchronizing classroom logistics or lesson design and delivery. The situation may be especially complex for students with information-processing difficulties. As a result, they may not know which direction to follow or which teacher to ask for assistance. Another consequence, often called "staff splitting," may occur when teachers do not get along: the old game of "he said, she said." Always savvy students can read an uncomfortable and tense relationship and may use a rift between teachers to manipulate a situation to their advantage. Here, of course, as in many families, one teacher says no to a request but the other teacher may say yes. The process of staff splitting may increase friction between the co-teachers. Thus, like parents, teachers must communicate with each other and ensure they are on the same page regarding interactions with children.

Effective communication is key to navigating professional relationships, whether teachers are thrown together or have time to get to know each other. The important consideration, as with family life and parents who have children's best interests at heart, is that most teachers enter the profession because they want to help children. To ultimately benefit students, then, this article presents problem-solving strategies to facilitate communication between co-teachers.

GETTING STARTED: THE RELATIONSHIP-BUILDING STAGE

Before beginning a co-teaching relationship, teachers first must know the meaning of co-teaching, as well as logistics involved with the process. Co-teaching is an instructional delivery model used to teach students with disabilities and those at risk of educational failure in the least restrictive, most productive, integrated classroom settings where both general and special educators share responsibility for planning, delivering, and evaluating instruction for all students (Arguelles, Hughes, & Schumm, 2000; Villa, Thousand, & Nevin, 2008). The practice provides teachers with an opportunity to share professional expertise. In most instances, general educators are considered *masters of content,* and special educators are viewed as *masters of access* (Villa et al., 2008). This delineation of competencies suggests that general educators have exclusive knowledge of curriculum, whereas special educators have sole knowledge of instructional processes for students who are identified as having disabilities or being at risk.

Unfortunately, attempts to merge the knowledge bases in co-teaching settings often causes confusion between teachers. Therefore, teaching partners need to communicate openly about issues that arise. The situation corresponds to newly married couples: Each person enters the relationship with diverse individual and cultural mores, which must be meshed to form a harmonious home. Co-teachers come together with dissimilar personal and professional values that they must identify, state, and combine in an effort to create positive academic and social climates for all students in their classroom settings.

In a recent study, Scruggs and colleagues (2007) found that co-teachers believe personal compatibility is the most important factor for co-teaching success. Thus, once teachers understand the definition of co-teaching they can begin to talk about the practicalities of their relationship. Teachers should first discuss their philosophy of education, specifically how they feel about teaching together in an inclusive classroom. Did they choose co-teaching, or was it chosen for them? If co-teaching was chosen for them, is it a process to which they can commit for a full school year?

Most teachers are willing to work together to benefit students for whom they share responsibility. In that regard, parity is the next issue they should address in their relationship. Parity implies equal status, or equality in substance. In a co-teaching relationship, parity suggests that all classroom responsibilities are shared equally, including instructional planning and delivery, discipline, grading, and collaborating with parents, among other tasks. Co-teachers' inability to discuss nitty-gritty details regarding shared classroom space, instructional noise levels, discipline, and daily chores often leads to unresolved issues that interfere with efforts to collaborate on behalf of students. Co-teachers need to discuss the basics of their partnership.

Ms. Happa's and Mr. Salvatore's hastily arranged relationship did not allow them an opportunity to talk about issues of parity and other fundamentals important to their professional association. Fortunately, they recognized the weakness in their relationship and rather than allow it to deteriorate, they decided to use a portion of their common planning time to address their roles and responsibilities. Some issues were easy to discuss, whereas others took a bit longer.

For example, they had common ideas about shared classroom space, discipline, daily chores, and communicating with parents. Mr. Salvatore was more than willing to share his classroom with Ms. Happa. He understood the need for both teachers to have separate desks or at least discrete places for their instructional materials and belongings. He also acknowledged that materials for a particular lesson should be stored in the classroom so that they were readily available for instruction. As a result, he arranged for a kidney-shaped table in the classroom for Ms. Happa to use during their lessons. The students were accustomed to Mr. Salvatore's disciplinary plan, so it was easy for Ms. Happa to follow his approach.

The teachers also decided to share daily chores, such as attendance taking and lunch count. Since Ms. Happa was not always in the room for attendance and lunch count activities, she performed other routine tasks during the day. For example, she often accompanied students to the cafeteria, thereby allowing Mr. Salvatore time to catch up with his e-mail messages.

Ms. Happa and Mr. Salvatore recognized the importance of parity in parent-teacher interactions and decided that they would communicate, jointly when possible, with all parents. As a matter of fact, on back-to-school night, they co-presented an overview of the school year and anticipated classroom events. This approach allowed parents to view both teachers as equal partners in the classroom.

Effective strategies for communicating with parents include (a) using various modes of communication, (b) inviting parents to visit or attend school events, (c) engaging families in curriculum planning, and (d) providing parents with resources to help their children succeed in school (Salend, 2010). Communication with parents is essential in building strong collaborative and co-teaching relationships, which ultimately benefit students. The advantage of a co-teaching partnership is that both teachers can communicate with parents to keep them informed of their children's academic and social growth and development. When this communication occurs, the teachers also learn about parental concerns and aspirations for their children.

Instructional noise is another issue to which co-teachers must attend. Classroom noise can become a problem if one teacher prefers teaching in a quiet setting and the other is comfortable with a noisy instructional environment. Figure 1 shows various types of classroom structures that many co-teachers use or consider as they plan (Friend & Bursuck, 2009).

Figure 1. Description of Co-Teaching Structures

1. **One Teach, One Observe**—when one teacher is responsible for whole group instruction while the other teacher observes the students and gathers information on their academic, social, and behavioral skills. This co-teaching structure allows co-teachers an opportunity to gather information about their students, and each other as well.

2. **Parallel Teaching**—when the co-teachers place the students into two equal groups and each teacher simultaneously teaches the same material to his or her small group. The benefit of this co-teaching structure is that it allows for increased teacher interaction and student participation as well as differentiation of instruction.

3. **Station Teaching**—when the co-teachers arrange the students into two or three equal groups, and the students rotate through each of the instructional stations. In this structure, the stations should not build on one another, but rather be nonsequential. The advantage of this co-teaching structure is that it also allows for increased teacher and student interactions.

4. **Alternative Teaching**—when one teacher teaches the whole group and the other teacher teaches a small group of students. The grouping for this structure should change according to students' needs. This co-teaching structure allows either teacher the opportunity to teach (e.g., remediation, preteaching, vocabulary development, and enrichment activities) for a short period of time.

5. **One Teach, One Assist**—when one teacher instructs the whole group and the other teacher assists individual students. The co-teaching structure allows the drifting teacher the opportunity to provide brief periods of individualized instruction to students who may be struggling with the academic content.

6. **Team Teaching**—when both teachers deliver instruction simultaneously to a large group of students. This structure affords the team teachers the chance to interact with the students. It also provides them with an opportunity to ask clarification questions of one another, thereby eliminating the potential confusion in instruction.

Mr. Salvatore believed that noisy classrooms were signs of collaborative learning; on the other hand, Ms. Happa believed that students should collaborate, but in a quiet manner. The easiest solution was to discuss acceptable noise levels within the classroom and to acknowledge that the intensity may increase or decrease, depending on the co-teaching structure (e.g., one teach, one observe; team-teaching; station teaching; one teach, one drift around the classroom).

Ms. Happa and Mr. Salvatore were able to accommodate this variability by planning instructional activities for both quiet and noisy classrooms. For example, a noisy lesson might be one in which the students work together using rulers to measure various items in the classroom. A quiet lesson might be one where students work in pairs to determine the meaning of a poem.

PLANNING: THE MARRIAGE/CO-TEACHING STAGE

After talking about minor details in their relationship, co-teaching partners must address the area of instruction. Most co-teachers, initially, were solo teachers and, like Mr. Salvatore, may not be comfortable sharing responsibility for instructional decisions. Therefore, it is essential for them to address issues related to curriculum planning and instruction. Critical topics to discuss include concerns such as who

- Plans and teaches the lessons.
- Prepares and organizes instructional materials.
- Chooses co-teaching structures that complement the lessons and students' abilities.
- Identifies assessment processes that determine students' acquisition of knowledge and ability to demonstrate skills and competencies.
- Grades assignments.

Such planning is crucial, especially for teachers who may experience arranged partnerships as a result of school district decisions and policies to implement RTI, which seeks to prevent academic failure in children who incur difficulty learning. RTI uses early instructional assistance, frequent measures of academic progress, and increasingly intense research-based instruction. As such, it requires general and special educators to collaborate actively to ensure implementation of lessons that address a wide array of instructional needs in general education classrooms and provide access to the general education curriculum for diverse learners (Murawski & Hughes, 2009).

As stated previously, special educators may be considered as the *masters of access* who at first have limited familiarity with curriculum and instructional materials. Consequently, they may assume several supportive roles in co-teaching settings, such as (a) providing back-up support to students, (b) teaching a component of the curriculum, and (c) team-teaching (Weiss & Lloyd, 2003). Special educators often assume more participatory instructional roles when they feel confident with curricular content.

Trent and colleagues (2003) found that a mutually satisfying co-teaching relationship emerges when teachers focus on technical aspects of planning, which ultimately benefit them, as well as the students. These teachers recognize the significance of "identifying their roles, responsibilities, sequences, and most importantly, who was going to do what" (p. 209). In addition, the teachers feel it is imperative to have structured planning time, rather than impromptu planning 5 minutes before class sessions. These delineations help define co-teaching relationships. When teachers are equal partners in instructional processes, they outwardly show few distinctions between them (Trent et al., 2003; Weiss & Lloyd, 2003). Therefore, it is imperative that co-teachers discuss planning and instructional techniques.

PROBLEM SOLVING: THE ONGOING RELATIONSHIP STAGE

What should teachers do when problems arise? As in other relationships, when things go wrong the partners need an opportunity to sit down and address issues in a structured manner. Similarly, co-teachers must discuss issues that confront them in a well-thought-out and orderly process. Luckily, co-teachers can find various problem-solving models (Berkeley & Ludlow, 2008; Sinclair, 1998) that can be modified to meet specific needs.

Sinclair's (1998) classic model is a seven-step process that includes (a) identifying issues; (b) developing alternative courses of action; (c) analyzing risks and benefits of each course of action; (d) choosing a course of action; (e) taking action; (f) evaluating results of the action; and (g) assuming responsibility for the consequences, correcting potentially negative consequences, or re-engaging in the decision-making process. Although some issues can be resolved rather quickly, others are more intricate and demand considerable time to disentangle them. A structured problem-solving model allows co-teaching partners to elucidate larger problems and hopefully avoid a breakup. The following scenario demonstrates how teachers may use Sinclair's problem-solving model in their co-teaching relationship.

After approximately a month of getting to know each other and the students, Ms. Happa and Mr. Salvatore hit a road bump in their teaching relationship. They had a solid foundation, yet Ms. Happa believed she could offer more to their professional association. As a result, she explained to Mr. Salvatore that she would like to contribute to instructional design and delivery. Although they had discussed various co-teaching models, Ms. Happa and Mr. Salvatore struggled with classroom implementation. They had a tendency to follow the "one teach, one assist" model, with Mr. Salvatore leading the lessons.

Mr. Salvatore enjoyed collaborating with Ms. Happa; however, he was uncertain about sharing instructional responsibility for the students. Ms. Happa explained to Mr. Salvatore that she earned a Master's Degree in Special Education and was knowledgeable about the curriculum, as well as appropriate instructional strategies.

The co-teachers were truly in a bind. They knew it was their responsibility to ensure a quality education for students. Yet, differences in how to provide instruction had the potential to interfere with the process. So, they decided to resolve their issues using Sinclair's (1998) model of problem solving.

Step 1: Identify the issues

Ms. Happa and Mr. Salvatore were having difficulty communicating. On the one hand, Mr. Salvatore wanted Ms. Happa in the classroom, but on the other, he did not want to share instructional design and delivery. Ms. Happa felt underappreciated because she was a competent teacher and wanted the opportunity to demonstrate her skills and knowledge. Although she tried many times, she could not get Mr. Salvatore to understand the "co" in co-teaching. She did not want to be in charge of his class; rather, she wanted to share instructional responsibilities.

Step 2: Develop alternative courses of action

Mr. Salvatore and Ms. Happa knew they shared the same goal: to afford success for all students. They just had difficulty figuring out how to achieve their goal. On the one hand, they could maintain the status quo and plod along in their disjointed efforts. On the other, they knew this approach was not appropriate and they needed alternative practices to work together. Ms. Happa and Mr. Salvatore decided to generate various solutions to their dilemma. After a lengthy discussion, they narrowed down their choices to three options. The first choice was to give up and end their relationship. The second alternative was to speak with the principal to see if she could ease the situation. The third option was for Mr. Salvatore to observe Ms. Happa co-teaching in another classroom.

Step 3: Analyze the risks and benefits of each course of action

Ms. Happa and Mr. Salvatore discussed each alternative. They decided that Option 1, giving up and ending the relationship, was not an option, especially because of the potential deleterious effects on the students. They were frustrated. They knew they had a solid foundation; they just hit a speed bump. They also knew they did not want to stay the course and end up hating co-teaching and each other. The risks of Option 1 were just too high; they had to identify another alternative.

Ms. Happa and Mr. Salvatore knew that they were both good teachers and there had to be a way to work together. They discussed Option 2, speaking with the principal. For Ms. Happa, the benefit of discussion with the principal was that she would receive support for her position. The principal was a firm believer in co-teaching. There were risks involved, however, in sharing the problem with the principal. First, both teachers had a good relationship with the principal and did not want to seem as though they could not solve the problem on their own.

Second, there was additional risk for Mr. Salvatore because he knew the principal was in favor of co-teaching to benefit students' education as well as teachers' professional development. He did not want to be viewed as an individual player rather than as a team member.

Finally, they discussed Option 3. Ms. Happa also co-taught with a fifth-grade teacher, and asked Mr. Salvatore if he would like to observe her co-teaching in the other setting. The benefit of this option is that Mr. Salvatore would have a concrete and positive example of a different co-teaching relationship.

Step 4: Choose a course of action

After considerable discussion, Ms. Happa and Mr. Salvatore chose the third alternative. Mr. Salvatore would observe Ms. Happa co-teaching in another setting.

Step 5: Take action

The following week during a preparatory period, Mr. Salvatore observed Ms. Happa co-teaching a fifth-grade mathematics lesson in which Ms. Happa and her co-teaching partner demonstrated two co-teaching structures. They began the lesson with parallel teaching, in which each teacher reviewed the morning work assignment. Next, she and the co-teacher taught alternatively. In this situation, Ms. Happa taught a small group of students while the co-teacher taught the larger group. The observation allowed Mr. Salvatore an opportunity to scrutinize Ms. Happa's teaching and learn that she could indeed teach.

Step 6: Evaluate results of the action

The next day, Ms. Happa and Mr. Salvatore discussed the observation. Ms. Happa explained the lesson components to Mr. Salvatore and asked if he had any questions. Mr. Salvatore told Ms. Happa that he was impressed, but he wanted to review the various co-teaching structures. He just was not sure how they would work in their shared setting. Ms. Happa explained the co-teaching structures (i.e., one teach, one observe; team-teaching; station teaching; and one teach, one drift) and offered examples of how each structure could work in their classroom, depending on the lesson content and students' instructional needs. (See Figure 2 for examples of how co-teaching structures may be used.)

Step 7: Assume responsibility for the consequences, correct potentially negative consequences, or re-engage in the decision-making process

After the observation, Mr. Salvatore decided to share responsibility for instructional design and delivery with Ms. Happa. Because he had observed a mathematics lesson, Mr. Salvatore decided to start co-teaching in mathematics. Ms. Happa was comfortable with his decision. They co-planned the lesson to ensure they were both engaged in the instructional processes. The lesson was a huge success without any hitches.

Figure 2. Examples of How to Use Co-Teaching Structures

1. **One Teach, One Observe** is an excellent strategy to implement during the first few weeks of school. It may be used during any lesson to determine which students are contributing to the lesson, as well as to identify students who need extra encouragement and support to contribute to class discussions. One teach, one observe also may be used to collect student data, monitor and support student behavior, and write and evaluate students' individualized education program objectives in preparation for meetings with parents and colleagues.

2. **Parallel Teaching** may be used in many different ways. The strength of the format is that it enables teachers to work with smaller numbers of students and to provide all students an opportunity for individualized and hands-on learning. Parallel teaching is an excellent format to use in science lessons, particularly those with experiments, especially because the teachers are working with a smaller number of students and have a better chance of controlling the variables.

3. **Station Teaching** is a good format to use in any curricular area. For example, in an English language arts lesson, the students, who are working in small groups, rotate through one of three stations. The teachers teach two stations (e.g., grammar and spelling) while other students work independently on narrative writing activities.

4. **Alternative Teaching** is an exceptional format to provide students with more intense and individualized instruction in a specific academic area. For example, many students have difficulty solving word problems. Therefore, one teacher can provide them with explicit instruction on solving word problems twice weekly for 15–20 minutes per session, while the other teacher works on other word problem-solving activities with the remaining students in the class.

5. **One Teach, One Assist** is an excellent strategy to check for student understanding. For example, during a math lesson, while one teacher is teaching, the other teacher can provide additional one-to-one assistance, such as reminding students about the first step to solve a problem, prompting students' use of a diagram to help understand the problem, or providing the definition of a concept to address students' difficulties and to ensure their understanding of the new material.

6. **Team Teaching** can be used in any academic subject, especially when presenting new material. In this instance, the co-teachers set up the lesson to question one another when a difficult concept is presented, thereby taking the pressure off of the students who may have difficulty understanding the new material. This structure also helps the teachers support each other as they present the material to ensure they addressed all steps and accurately reinforced the concepts.

Note. Adapted from "Creating optimal opportunities to learn mathematics: Blending co-teaching structures with research-based practices," by J. M. Sileo & D. van Garderen (2010), *TEACHING Exceptional Children,* *42*(3), 14–21. Copyright 2010 by the Council for Exceptional Children.

As an aside, Ms. Happa and Mr. Salvatore have been co-teaching successfully for 8 years and advocate for the process among their colleagues.

FINAL THOUGHTS

The beginning stage of any co-teaching relationship is similar to the initial aspects of any dating relationship. At first, the relationship is great, and the partners are blissful and happy. As time evolves, however, newly formed relationships need to be nurtured to create a stronger relationship, because performing as a team is hard work, if it is to be successful and long lasting. New couples in any relationship often argue about simple things, such as leaving the cap off the toothpaste tube or which of the partners is responsible for doing laundry, vacuuming, or cooking. The same can be said for new co-teaching partners. The teachers may disagree about leaving the lid off the whiteboard marker or putting away instructional materials at the end of the day.

In either marriage or co-teaching, the key to success is compromise and collaboration. All co-teachers must be flexible for their relationship to flourish. Therefore, co-teaching partners must communicate throughout the relationship to ensure the relationship focuses on what is most important in co-teaching—children's academic and social growth and development.

REFERENCES

Arguelles, M. E., Hughes, M. T., & Schumm, J. S. (2000). Co-teaching: A different approach to inclusion. *Principal, 79*(4), 48, 50–51.

Berkeley, T. R., & Ludlow, B. L. (2008). Ethical dilemmas in rural special education: A call for a conversation about the ethics of practice. *Rural Special Education Quarterly, 27*(1/2), 3–9.

Friend, M., & Bursuck, W. D. (2009). *Including students with special needs: A practical guide for classroom teachers* (5th ed.). Columbus, OH: Merrill.

Murawski, W. W., & Hughes, C. E. (2009). Response to intervention, collaboration, and co-teaching: A logical combination for successful systemic change. *Preventing School Failure, 53*, 267–277. doi: 10.32001PSFL.53.4.267-277

Salend, S. J. (2010). *Creating inclusive classrooms: Effective and reflective practices* (7th ed.). Upper Saddle River, NJ: Pearson.

Scruggs, T. E., Mastropieri, M. A., & McDuffie, K. A. (2007). Co-teaching in inclusive classrooms: A metasynthesis of qualitative research. *Exceptional Children, 47*, 392–416.

Sileo, J. M., & van Garderen, D. (2010). Creating optimal opportunities to learn mathematics: Blending co-teaching structures with research-based practices. *TEACHING Exceptional Children, 42*(3), 14–21.

Sinclair, C. (1998). Nine unique features of the Canadian code of ethics for psychologists. *Canadian Psychology/Psychologie Canadienne, 39*, 167–176. doi: 10.1037/h0086805

Trent, S. C., Driver, B. L., Wood, M. H., Parrott, P. S., Martin, T. F., & Smith W. G. (2003). Creating and sustaining a special education/general education partnership: A story of evolution, change, and uncertainty. *Teaching and Teacher Education, 19*, 203–219. doi: 10.1016/S0742-051X(02)0014X

Villa, R. A., Thousand, J. S., & Nevin, A. I. (2008). *A guide to co-teaching: Practical tips for facilitating student learning* (2nd ed.). Thousand Oaks, CA: Corwin Press.

Weiss, M. P., & Lloyd, J. (2003). Conditions for co-teaching: Lessons from a case study. *Teacher Education and Special Education, 26*, 27–41. doi: 10.1177/088840640302600104

Note: The names of the co-teachers in this article are pseudonyms.

Originally published in *TEACHING Exceptional Children,* Vol. 43, No. 5, pp. 32–38.

2

50 Ways to Keep Your Co-Teacher: Strategies for Before, During, and After Co-Teaching

Wendy W. Murawski and Lisa Dieker

General education teacher (overheard in the hallway): "Oh yeah, I used to have a special educator working with me in the classroom . . . but I do not know what happened to her!"

We know! Although co-teaching may be here to stay, co-teachers themselves do not always stick around. As researchers, teacher educators, and co-teachers ourselves, we are keenly aware of the issues related to obtaining—and more important, keeping—good co-teaching teams. In fact, educators frequently relate co-teaching to a marriage; unfortunately, research clearly indicates that many co-teaching marriages result in struggle, separation, or even divorce. This article uses humor and mnemonics to highlight the keys to effective co-teaching that research and literature have identified. Our purpose is to clarify the critical factors necessary for developing and maintaining a successful co-teaching team.

CLARIFYING CO-TEACHING

Co-teaching is a service delivery option designed to address the needs of students in an inclusive classroom by having a general education teacher and a special service provider (e.g., special education teacher, speech/language pathologist, Title I teacher) teach together in the same classroom to meet the needs of individual students. For true co-teaching to occur, both professionals must "co-plan, co-instruct, and co-assess a diverse group of students in the same general education classroom" (Murawski, 2005, p.10). With the ongoing move toward inclusive education (wherein educators teach students with special needs in the general education classroom), co-teaching is a service delivery option that educators increasingly use to meet the needs of both teachers and students (Scruggs, Mastropieri, & McDuffie, 2007). Although not all educators will experience co-teaching, more teachers than ever before are looking for tools to help make them more successful (see box, "What Does the Literature Say About Co-Teaching?").

To rectify the problems associated with co-teaching, co-teachers should consider the following suggestions for before, during, and after co-teaching. Because many of these tips overlap (for example, issues related to planning occur before, during, and after co-teaching is already in place), those interested in co-teaching should read the entire article rather than using it as a step-by-step checklist. Also, the authors have based all tips on their years of experience, experiences of other co-teachers, and research conducted on co-teaching. Thus, some of the hints are evidence-based practices already supported in the research, whereas others are practices suggested by experienced co-teachers. Following each tip is a question to ask yourself, your co-teacher, or other stakeholders. We hope that the catchy phrases will help ensure that you keep right on co-teaching and finding success for both teachers and students.

BEFORE CO-TEACHING

1. *Hop on the bus, Gus.* Volunteer to co-teach before anyone tells you to do so. Inclusive education is not going away. Schools increasingly require that teachers collaborate, many by some form of co-teaching, because of the changes in the Individuals With Disabilities Education Improvement Act (IDEA) of 2004 and changes related to the highly qualified component of No Child Left Behind (2002). Get ahead of the curve by volunteering and choosing a compatible partner before someone tells you that you must co-teach.

   Ask yourself: Have I stepped up to the plate and volunteered yet?

2. *Talk to the boss, Ross.* Administrators can help provide materials, resources, improved schedules, and more. Furnish them with articles that clarify co-teaching, and discuss with them your particular needs. Some resources that you may find helpful in sharing with administrators include Boscardin (2005), Murawski and Lochner (2007), Rea et al. (2002), Rea (2005), Walther-Thomas (1997), and Wilson (2005).

   Ask each other: Have you considered what you need to create or improve your co-teaching situation and how those needs will affect student outcomes? How will you communicate those needs to your administrator?

> ## What Does the Literature Say About Co-Teaching?
>
> Less than 10 years ago, little research on co-teaching existed (Murawski & Swanson, 2001); however, recent studies have found that it can be a very effective method for meeting students' needs (e.g., Magiera, Smith, Zigmond, & Gebauer, 2005; Murawski, 2006; Rea, McLaughlin, & Walther-Thomas, 2002; Scruggs, Mastropieri, & McDuffie, 2007). However, as with any paradigm shift, change is difficult and barriers are common. Teachers have reported a variety of frustrations with co-teaching; they include lack of training (Mastropieri et al., 2005); lack of administrative support (Dieker, 2001; Rea, 2005); and a lack of parity in the classroom (Dieker & Murawski, 2003; Spencer, 2005). Dr. Lynne Cook, a noted expert on co-teaching, clarified that "co-teaching is not simply having two teachers in a classroom with one acting as a glorified paraprofessional or an in-class tutor for one or two students" (Spencer, p. 297), and yet that is exactly what many teachers complain is occurring (Weiss & Lloyd, 2002).

3. *Get trained, Layne.* Co-teachers frequently cite the need for training in collaboration, co-teaching, and differentiation strategies (e.g., Mastropieri et al., 2005). Seizing opportunities for staff development in-service training and workshops is helpful, as is reading books and articles that focus on the collaborative relationship in inclusive classrooms. Ask whether you and your co-teacher can attend a workshop on co-teaching or inclusion together. (Speakers' bureaus like the Bureau of Education and Research [www.ber.org] can provide high-quality staff development.)

   Ask your administrator: How can you help ensure that we are well trained in co-teaching before we begin?

4. *Make a new plan, Stan.* Recognize the importance of trying things in a new way. Beninghof (2003) states that one of the most common mistakes of co-teaching is that neither educator is willing to "loosen the corset" and be more flexible in this new relationship. Both teachers need to approach this new relationship with willingness to let go of control a bit and try new things.

   Ask each other: Are you game to try something new? What "sacred cows" are you willing to sacrifice?

5. *Keep the numbers low, Joe.* Putting two full classes together is not the answer. One of the benefits of co-teaching is the lower student-teacher ratio (Friend & Cook, 2003). A good rule of thumb is to keep to the natural proportions of individuals with disabilities in society—about 20%. If you need to cluster more, up to 30% of the students might have a disability, but try to avoid having a class in which all 30% represent the same type of disability (e.g., a class in which 10% have behavioral disabilities and 20% have learning disabilities, rather than a class in which 30% have learning disabilities). Too great a number of students with learning or behavioral challenges jeopardizes the benefits that you are hoping to see.

Make sure that your inclusive class does not become a place for all struggling students—that is, in essence a special education class with only a few general education students.

Ask each other: How many students in our co-taught class have identified disabilities? How many are at risk, are English language learners, are gifted, or are otherwise exceptional?

6. *Prepare the class, Cass.* Just as you prepare to work together as a team, make sure that you have prepared students to start working in a more inclusive setting. Co-teaching "is not the only effective approach, and it is not necessarily the best approach for all kids" (L. Cook, as cited in Spencer, 2005, p. 297). Consider which students need to be in a co-taught class, and then consider how you will adequately prepare them for this transition.

Ask the parents: Is your child prepared to be in a co-taught general education class? What services and adaptations need to be in place to ensure his or her success?

7. *Inform the parents, Clarence.* Send a letter home to all parents to inform them that two teachers will be in the classroom. It is not necessary to state that one of you is a special educator and one is a general educator. Simply state that two credentialed teachers will equally share in planning, instructing, and assessing the whole class (Murawski, 2005).

Ask each other: Who will take the lead in parental contact, or will we divide this task as a team?

8. *Share the news, Suz.* Be certain that others in the school are aware that you are co-teaching. This preparation helps ensure that administrators do not call either teacher away on a regular basis for an emergency meeting, to help with a behavior problem, or to talk to a parent. Parity is critical, as is the consistent presence of both teachers in the class. Co-teachers often report that they are unable to depend on each other for planning and instruction because one is often out of the class for a variety of reasons (e.g., for IEP meetings, for behavioral issues, or to substitute in another class).

Ask yourselves: Do the students see you both as the teacher, or do they see one as the "real teacher" and the other as an aide who is in and out?

Ask the administrator: Are you prepared to treat us both as real teachers in the room and avoid calling the special educator out for various reasons?

9. *Don't need to be coy, Roy.* Make sure to communicate your pet peeves, preferences, strengths, and weaknesses with your co-teacher before the start of the semester. Talking about these preferences will help avoid personality conflicts and other miscommunications. Use the SHARE worksheet in Murawski and Dieker (2004) to facilitate conversation about important areas of teaching on which you will need to agree.

Ask each other: When can we sit down and review our responses on the SHARE worksheet?

10. *Drop off the key, Lee.* Be willing to share all materials. To ensure parity, do not allow students to think that one teacher owns the materials or room because the other always has to ask permission to use items. Instead, demonstrate parity by creating common materials and space and putting both names on the board, the roster, the report cards, and any communications home.

Ask yourselves: If we look around the room and at our materials, do we emphasize one teacher over the other? What can we do to remedy that situation?

11. *Commit to co-plan, Dan.* Planning together is the most important part of co-teaching (Murawski, 2005). Before you enter the co-teaching relationship, talk to your potential partners about how you will identify time to get together to co-plan, especially when you are new to co-teaching. Dieker (2001) demonstrated through research that veteran co-teachers only need about 10 minutes to plan for a week; however, those teachers had previously co-taught. In new situations, overplanning is better than underplanning. Ideas for finding time to co-plan are available in Murawski and Dieker (2004). Two excellent resources to help structure co-planning to make time and ensure consistency are *The Co-Teaching Lesson Plan Book* (Dieker, 2006) and the Co-Teaching Solutions System (CTSS) Teachers' Toolbox (www.coteachsolutions.com; Murawski & Lochner, 2007).

Ask the administrator: Are you willing to support our efforts by purchasing *The Co-Teaching Lesson Plan Book* or CTSS Toolbox and helping us find time to meet regularly to co-plan?

12. *Each take a piece, Reece.* One of the best things about co-teaching is the opportunity to share—responsibility, accountability, workload, and fun (Cook & Friend, 1995)! Letting teachers know that they will have someone else to help with planning, obtaining materials, grading, and other chores is one of the best ways to attract interest in co-teaching.

Ask each other: How will we break up the load so that we both will benefit?

13. *Work where you are strong, Wong, and address where you are weak, Zeke.* Being aware of each other's strengths and weaknesses is mandatory. Be honest, and share with each other whether you are a procrastinator or a type-A control freak. Discuss whether you love or hate to plan, grade, and take care of discipline and other aspects of instruction. Although special educators do not need to be content experts, they need to be willing to expand on their content knowledge if that is an area of weakness, especially at the secondary level. General educators may share that they feel comfortable with the content and standards but may be less familiar with

individualizing strategies or ways to make content accessible to students who are struggling.

Ask each other: What are your strengths and weaknesses, and how do they affect your teaching? (Perhaps you will find that you two will truly complement each other. If not, you should discuss compromises.)

14. *It's OK to be trendy, Wendy.* Read current material on brain-based learning, and offer some "teaching to the brain" tricks as your role in the co-taught class. Be aware of other strategies, tools, and techniques that come from a variety of sources (e.g., English language learning seminars, as well as literacy and mathematics coaches); and be willing to use whatever might make a difference in student engagement and learning.

Ask specialists in your district: Can you share any new strategies with us so that we can help our students increase their academic, behavioral, and learning skills?

15. *Establish clear rules, Jules.* The co-teachers need to discuss the way that each person deals with behavioral issues before beginning co-teaching. Check to be certain that your rules are clear enough that you can provide consequences in less than 3 seconds and that you both are consistently acknowledging positive behavior and not merely reinforcing bad behavior.

Ask each other: What are our roles and preferences related to behavior in the co-teaching setting?

16. *Always be fair, Cher.* In a strong co-teaching climate, both teachers clearly understand that fair means that everyone gets what he or she needs (and that fair does not mean that everyone gets the same or equal things). In inclusive classrooms where teachers are clear about fairness from the beginning and share their philosophy with students, this issue never arises. However, if the co-teachers do not share this concept early, students and teachers will struggle to understand why some students receive different support than others.

Ask yourselves: Do you both hold similar philosophies about fairness? If not, you need to discuss this issue in the first days of planning. This topic can make or break your relationship.

17. *They are "our" kids, Sid.* Effective co-teachers always talk about "our" kids, not "yours and mine." They do not differentiate students by label or assign them to one teacher or the other. Special education teachers or paraprofessionals do not hover over the students with IEPs but are helping all students. Consider how you can include students with special needs; is it that they are merely physically present, or do you and the students truly include them in the social and academic environment?

Ask each other and any paraprofessionals in the room: How have we ensured that we meet students' needs without adults hovering over them or placing them in small segregated groups in the back of the classroom?

18. *Go to the Web, Jeb.* Be certain to check for available resources on the Web (such as www.powerof2.org, www.specialconnections.ku.edu, www .2TeachLLC.com) to find tools to help you with your co-teaching. Also, blogs (online journals) can enable teachers to talk collaboratively across schools and across the country.

    Ask any available special education or technology specialists: What Web-based resources have you found to help support our co-teaching relationship?

19. *Share your needs, Reed.* Make sure before you start that you discuss the "big ideas" that relate to content and curricula, as well as the individual needs of students with disabilities. Typically, the general educator takes the lead on sharing the content, whereas the special educator takes the lead on sharing individual student information; but both teachers' information should be equally valued. One teacher does not "trump" the other in power. If this planning can happen before you start to co-teach together, then you will have a clearer understanding of how skills, curricula, and students' needs complement or clash with one another.

    Ask the general educator: What curricula will we cover during the first semester?

    Ask the special educator: What information do we have on the individual students so that we can better meet their needs within the context of our class?

20. *Hit the books, Brooks.* A plethora of available research describes the ways that children learn. For example, one of our favorites is the work of pediatrician Dr. Mel Levine. Levine has written groundbreaking work that does not rely on labels or disability categories but that helps educators and parents gain more knowledge about how children learn. Both co-teachers can read *A Mind at a Time* (Levine, 2002); go through Schools Attuned training, which is a weeklong intensive training program on neurodevelopmental constructs and identifying students' strengths to improve all areas of need; or visit www.allkindsofminds.org so that they can begin to use similar language and strategies when working with struggling learners. Other excellent resources include those of Dr. Robert Brooks (www .drrobertbrooks.com), Richard Lavoie, and Carol Ann Tomlinson, as well as Margo Mastropieri and Thomas Scruggs.

    Ask your administrator: Can you obtain copies of recommended resources for us to read or send us to specialized training?

21. *Talk about the grade, Wade.* Too many times, grading becomes an area of conflict between co-teachers. Before the start of the semester, teachers should talk about the variety of grading options and determine the best collaborative option. After deciding, they should share any adaptations to grading with individual students and their parents. An excellent resource for a discussion of various grading practices is Struyk et al. (1995).

Ask each other: With what types of grading adaptations are you comfortable? With what adaptations would you not be comfortable?

During Co-Teaching

22. *Check your HALO, Jaylo.* Throughout your lesson planning and instruction, always check with each other that you have adequately addressed all learners in the class. You need to include students who are **H**(igh achieving), **A**(verage achieving), **L**(ow achieving), and **O**(ther), (Murawski, 2005). If you have addressed your HALO, you know that you will have a differentiated lesson designed to improve learning for all students. Another excellent resource for helping with lesson planning is "Building a Strong BASE of Support for All Students Through Coplanning" (Hawbaker, Balong, Buckwalter, & Runyon, 2001).

    Ask your administrator: If you look at our lesson plans, can you clearly see that we address our HALO so that the lesson is appropriately differentiated?

23. *Walk the talk, Jacques.* Educators often impress on students that learning to work together is a lifelong skill; co-teaching gives you a chance to model that skill. Consider how you can demonstrate to students that you are equals in the classroom and that you can sometimes agree to disagree. Use the communication and collaboration skills that Friend and Cook (2003) recommend.

    Ask the students: When we as co-teachers disagree, how do you think that we should resolve our issues? What specific strategies can we use to better communicate with each other?

24. *Circulate the room, June.* When one person is leading, the other person should be moving throughout the room and making sure that the lesson is meeting the needs of all students (Friend & Cook, 2003). While one teacher is instructing the class, the other should not be grading papers, making copies, or catching up on individualized education programs (IEPs; Murawski, 2005). Discuss your comfort level with movement in the classroom.

    Ask each other: What are some actions that one of us can do while the other is leading an activity or giving a lecture?

25. *Slip out the back, Jack.* A true benefit of co-teaching is the ability to take a much-needed bathroom break. As long as it does not become a habit or a way to escape class, the option of leaving one teacher in the room to facilitate class while the other runs to the bathroom is a basic, but very valued, benefit to co-teaching.

    Ask each other: What nonverbal sign can we give to the other teacher that indicates we are desperate for a quick break?

26. *Give the brain a break, Jake.* The latest brain research emphasizes the need for "brain breaks" every 10 to 12 minutes for students to chunk

knowledge. This type of brain break is especially important in a lecture type of setting. Monitor each other to see whether you are doing activities that allow students to process and chunk information.

Ask each other: Do we see the students self-initiating their own brain breaks (e.g., putting heads on desks, doodling, or passing notes)? If so, we need to change what we are doing and discuss how to make sure that we are providing teacher-initiated brain breaks instead.

27. *Get them together, Heather.* In all settings, students need to feel valued. At the same time, teachers need to use classroom practices that are evidence-based. Cooperative learning has strong research support as an effective classroom practice (Johnson, Johnson, & Stanne, 2000), and it also provides opportunities for positive peer interactions. When done well, students with disabilities not only receive help but also have the chance to assist their peers in learning.

    Ask the students: Why do you think that we sometimes place you in groups to work? What are the benefits and challenges to this type of activity? Do you enjoy it, and do you learn from it? How can we improve this cooperative style?

28. *Create a great climate, Violet.* Creating a positive climate for all students is critical. When teachers use such tools as cooperative learning or class-wide peer tutoring, they need to be certain to allow students to assess their own behavior. Tools such as those that Dieker and Ousley (2006) suggest can be very helpful in allowing students to assess group behavior.

    The bottom line is for the teachers to ask each other: What did we do today to create an environment that was accepting of all students?

29. *Repeat and clarify, Ty.* As all educators know, repetition aids retention. This strategy is helpful for all students, not just those with disabilities. Co-teachers can collaborate so that they can write information on the board, repeat directions, and provide verbal prompts throughout the lesson. These proactive strategies help ensure that fewer reactive strategies (like pulling out or reteaching) are necessary.

    Ask each other as you review your lesson: How does today's lesson meet the visual, auditory, kinesthetic, processing, and behavioral needs of students?

30. *Take a group, Snoop.* Instead of assuming that all students can learn in the large-group setting, do not be afraid to take a small group out to learn. As long as you do not always pull the same students out for reteaching (in essence, stigmatizing them the same way that a pullout class would), the use of a small group can be very beneficial. In addition, co-teachers can also take out a heterogeneous group of students who might need more challenges.

    Ask each other: On the basis of the content that we need to teach, do any of the students need reteaching, preteaching, or enrichment?

31. *Boring is bad, Lad.* Differentiating instruction helps ensure that you are meeting more students' needs (Tomlinson, 2005) and can involve more interesting activities than straight lecture. Certainly, coming up with differentiated and motivating lessons is much easier with two people. Two teachers means that two people can help figure out how to "shake up" the lesson and ensure maximum student engagement.

    Ask each other: What are we doing to make sure that the class is not boring?

    Then ask the students (if you dare): Is this class boring? If so, what are your suggestions for making it more interesting—while still ensuring that we teach the content adequately?

32. *Plan to laugh, Taff.* Make laughter a part of your classroom practice. Laughter reduces stress and can help encode learning. Think about being the cartoon or joke-of-the-day person. Having another adult in the room who understands your jokes is nice, but the real challenge is finding humor that students understand.

    Ask yourselves: How have we incorporated laughter or emotion into our lesson for today?

33. *Keep standards high, Sy.* Standards-based instruction is one of the stated benefits of inclusive education; all students can have access to grade-level curriculum (Thurlow, 2002). Do not water work down just because a student has a label. Consider identifying methods of teaching to the standards that also enable students with special needs to succeed; one resource, for example, is the Kansas University Content Enhancement and Unit Planning strategy (www.specialconnections.ku.edu). This type of resource can help take content and break it down into accessible parts for all the students in the room.

    Ask yourselves: What strategies are we using for the whole class that will really help struggling students at the same time? Also, are we basing all accommodation and modification decisions on the needs of the students rather than on their labels?

34. *Ensure success, Jess.* When you are in the co-teaching setting, remember to plan for the range of needs in the classroom, including students who have English language needs, students who are slow learners, students who have disabilities, students who are gifted, and students who fall into multiple or other categories. Remember to think about each student as an individual and consider the type of scaffolding or support that he or she might need so that you are challenging all students. Each student has the right to be successful in your class.

    Ask each other: Which students do we not seem to reach effectively?

    Ask parents: Do you believe that the class is meeting your child's needs? If not, do you have suggestions or strategies so that we can help ensure success for your child?

35. *Help students pay attention, Christian.* Students with attention issues in the classroom need to have stimulation that can help them focus on the most important task—your teaching. One of the benefits noted in the research is that teachers in co-teaching settings have to do less direct classroom management simply because two teachers are in the classroom (Murawski, 2006). However, for some students, proximity will not be enough to keep their attention.

    Ask each other: Have we incorporated activities of high interest and movement into our co-taught lessons? Are our kinesthetic learners able to stay focused?

36. *Break out the toys, Joy.* Many teacher-friendly manipulatives are available for students. They hold students' attention, make a lesson kinesthetic, and help with active learning. Although teachers may not be able to buy all the materials they want on their own, consider talking to other teachers about sharing materials, asking district and school administrators what is available, and seeing whether community stakeholders will provide financial support (many local businesses have surplus that they are happy to share).

    Ask your administrators: Can we get Wikki Stix (www.wikkistix.com), Gelboards (www.gelboard.com), Play-Doh, or erasable highlighters to use in our lessons? What types of materials are available for us to use?

37. *Take a time out, Scout.* If a student or group of students is getting on your nerves, communicate your frustration to your co-teacher by using a non-verbal signal and switching roles instead of blowing up at them. Being able to take a self time-out from kids for a moment or being able to switch student groups is another benefit of co-teaching.

    Ask yourself: Have you ever had a moment when you just knew you were going to lose it? Won't it be nice to have a chance to avoid that situation?

38. *Don't disappear, Dear.* Last-minute IEPs, behavioral problems, and parent concerns can pull special educators out of the co-taught classroom on a regular basis. Some administrators even have special educators substitute for another teacher's class when a substitute is unavailable. That strategy affects the continuity of instruction, impairs the teachers' planning, and makes general educators begin to believe that they cannot depend on the co-teacher to be there for instruction. Administrators and both teachers must commit to a continuing relationship for at least the semester (preferably the year) to provide continuity to students. In addition, administrators and other personnel must understand that they should not call either teacher out of class unless a true emergency has occurred.

    Ask each other and the administrators: Are we all committed to make this work? Do we really understand what that commitment means? How can we communicate this to others?

39. *Don't be late, Nate.* Even when teachers are co-teaching with multiple people and going to separate classes, it is important to start the instruction with both teachers present and on time. Their collective presence sets a tone of parity and allows the class to start immediately.

    Ask each other: Is tardiness an issue? What are our options to remedy this problem?

40. *Play some games, James.* Multiuse games (like Jeopardy, Bingo, and Who Wants to Be a Millionaire) are great ways to reinforce concepts in an inclusive classroom. Students become more motivated to learn when they are enjoying themselves. Two teachers in the room can facilitate and control games more easily than one teacher.

    Ask students: What games do you like to play? If we include these activities as an instructional method, do we have your commitment to interact appropriately? What does that mean to you?

41. *Change your approach, Coach.* Novice co-teachers often report mainly using a "one teach, one support" approach in the classroom (Weiss & Lloyd, 2002). Although that approach is understandable, students do not receive the benefits of having two credentialed teachers in the classroom when co-teachers use that approach. In addition, the role of the support teacher becomes more like that of a paraprofessional (Scruggs, et al., 2007; Weiss & Lloyd). For improved student outcomes, it pays to do more regrouping and try a variety of approaches and strategies to make the most of co-teaching (Cook & Friend, 1995).

    Ask yourselves: How often do we regroup students? Can we look at our lesson plans and see that we frequently vary our instructional approaches, rather than merely taking turns leading the lesson?

42. *Address their MI, Guy.* As a co-teaching team, consider how you can plan lessons that address the various strengths of the learners in your classroom. Educators too often focus on the use of sight and sound (e.g., lecture and overheads), yet these are the two areas in which many students with disabilities have limited skills. Therefore, think about how to address in your lessons all the multiple intelligences (MIs), as well as the various ways that students learn (Stanford, 2003).

    Ask the specialists in your district: Does anyone have more information on MI theory, and can you provide us with subject-specific strategies that we can use with our students?

43. *Address different learning styles, Giles.* Recognize that only about 50% of students have visual and auditory learning style strengths; the other 50% are typically kinesthetic/tactile learners. Teachers tend to be visual and auditory learners and continue to teach in the way that others taught them. This method of teaching, however, does not match with many of the students' learning styles in inclusive classrooms.

Ask yourselves: How have we ensured that we are teaching these students in a way that connects with their learning styles? Have we considered our own learning styles and how they affect our teaching styles?

44. *Don't depart, Art.* Pulling students with IEPs away for testing is not always necessary. Instead, allow all students to determine their learning style preferences, and let those preferences identify how you will test them. Doing assessments in a variety of ways can allow students to demonstrate their learning instead of penalizing them for having a disability. Look to the work of Carol Ann Tomlinson (e.g., Tomlinson, 2005) for a plethora of ways to differentiate by product (in addition to differentiating by content and by process).

    Ask students: On the basis of your own learning style, would you prefer that someone read this test to you or would you prefer to read it yourself? Everyone can choose his or her own method for this particular assessment.

45. *Record your voice, Joyce.* Using listening centers with tape recorders and headsets enables co-teachers to allow some students to work independently (e.g., in station teaching) while the teachers work with smaller groups. Tape recorders also are a perfect solution for students who need tests read to them, since the co-teachers do not need to read a test multiple times for multiple students. Also, make sure that your administrators know that you are using this strategy and that students are not merely chillin' out to their favorite band.

    Ask administrators: Are funds available for purchasing blank tapes and tape recorders for us?

AFTER CO-TEACHING HAS BEGUN

46. *Collect some data, Jada.* Having two teachers in the room allows you both to collect data on student achievement, problem and positive behaviors, and areas of need. Curriculum-based assessments, benchmark tests, Dynamic Indicators of Basic Early Literacy Skills (DIBELS), attendance information, data on academic engaged time, and class grades are types of data that you can collect to demonstrate the success—or lack thereof—of co-teaching teams. Make sure to work together to collect information so that you can make decisions on the basis of data rather than on the basis of opinion or emotion. An excellent resource for collecting concrete data on co-teaching actions is the Co-Teaching Solutions Systems (CTSS) Observation System (www.coteachsolutions.com), created for observers to document what is occurring in the co-taught classroom. A highlight of the CTSS Observation System is a self-survey that enables co-teachers to self-assess and then electronically compare their responses with the observers' feedback.

Ask each other: What data are important to us? How will we collect our data, and who will do the collecting?

47. *Remember to evaluate, Mate.* Having others provide feedback on your co-teaching, as well as conducting your own self-evaluations, is important. Administrators or other observers may want to start with the questions provided in Wilson (2005) for outside evaluations. These questions include the following:

    • Is the role of each teacher meaningful?

    • Are co-teachers using strategies to promote success with all students in the classroom?

    • Does evidence indicate that successful learning is occurring in the class?

    Although these questions provide a structure for outside observers, co-teachers should agree on a standard process and time to evaluate their own teaching and the co-teaching relationship.

    After you have a standard date on your calendar (at least once a month), we recommend asking two simple questions.

    Ask each other: Is what we are doing good for both of us? If not, what are we doing that we could change so that we both are happy with the relationship? Is our co-teaching good for all students in our class? If not, what can we do to ensure that all students are benefiting from our collaboration?

48. *Avoid any blame, Ame.* If any areas are not working, be sure that you and your co-teacher deal with them yourselves. Venting to others in the teachers' lounge is a sure way to ruin a potentially good co-teaching relationship and does not remedy the situation. Instead, commit to having fair and open discussions only with each other about what is and what is not working.

    Ask each other: How do you prefer feedback, especially when one of us is not pleased? What type of a plan can we create to evaluate and address issues as they arise?

49. *Share your success, Bess.* Be certain that you tell everyone who will listen what is working. Co-teaching often spreads at a school when teachers hear about the benefits and successes of students and faculty. An inclusive school should include all faculty, staff, students, and parents; it should not rely on only a few people who collaborate successfully.

    Ask district personnel: How can we share our successes across the district? Are there other co-teaching teams with whom we can communicate to share tips, strategies and successes?

50. *Let the celebration begin, Vin.* As previously mentioned, educators often compare co-teaching with a marriage. If you and your co-teacher follow these simple 50 tips, you will be ready to pour the champagne and look

forward to celebrating an anniversary. Congratulations on this wonderful collaboration—we knew you could do it!

What question should you ask each other: Would you do it all over again? Of course!

REFLECTION

With each of these tips to keep your co-teacher, we provided questions— questions for you to ask yourselves, your co-teachers, your administrators, your students, your students' parents, and other personnel in the school and district. Asking these questions helps ensure ongoing communication and treatment integrity (that is, the assurance that any intervention is implemented as intended). Too often, administrators throw co-teachers into an arranged co-teaching relationship; and the co-teachers focus on their resentment that no one asked them for their opinion, that they were not trained, or that they do not know the content or the special needs of the students the way that the other educator does. The authors sincerely hope that our tips and questions can enable co-teachers to avoid negative relationships and make the most of any situation. By doing so, they can focus on the positive experiences that they as teachers are receiving and the academic, behavioral, and social benefits that the students are experiencing.

We have used tips that are based on research-based and practical strategies to offer ways for co-teachers to obtain, maintain, or even improve their current collaborative relationships. Co-teachers can and should reflect on each question and determine where they need to do some problem solving. Facilitators or administrators engaged in supporting co-teaching can use these questions to guide their own co-teaching staff development.

Ultimately, in our own reflections, three important components to successful co-teaching emerged that permeate all 50 tips. For each of the previously mentioned suggestions, please also keep in mind the following:

- Be willing to try new things.
- Be willing to be equals.
- Be willing to listen—to each other, to students, to parents, and to others.

We are certain that those who approach co-teaching with a positive can-do attitude—just like any other aspect of teaching—will experience the truly wonderful benefits that co-teaching has to offer . . . and better yet, that the students will as well!

REFERENCES

Beninghof, A. (2003). *Co-teaching that works: Effective strategies for working together in today's inclusive classrooms.* Bellevue, WA: Bureau of Education and Research.

Boscardin, M. L. (2005). The administrative role in transforming secondary schools to support inclusive evidence-based practices. *American Secondary Education, 33*(3), 21-32.

Cook, L., & Friend, M. (1995). Co-teaching: Guidelines for creating effective practices. *Focus on Exceptional Children, 28*(3), 1–15.

Dieker, L., & Ousley, D. (2006). Speaking the same language: Bringing together highly qualified secondary English and special education teachers. *TEACHING Exceptional Children Plus.* Retrieved January 3, 2008, from http://escholarship.bc.edu /education/tecplus/vol2/iss4/art3

Dieker, L. A. (2001). What are the characteristics of "effective" middle and high school co-taught teams? *Preventing School Failure, 46*(1), 14–25.

Dieker, L. A. (2006). *The co-teaching lesson plan book: Academic year version.* Whitefish Bay, WI: Knowledge by Design.

Dieker, L. A., & Murawski, W. W. (2003). Co-teaching at the secondary level: Unique issues, current trends, and suggestions for success. *The High School Journal 86*(4), 1–13.

Friend, M., & Cook, L. (2003). *Interactions: Collaboration skills for school professionals* (4th ed.). White Plains, NY: Longman.

Hawbaker, B. W., Balong, M., Buckwalter, S., & Runyon, S. (2001). Building a strong BASE of support for all students through coplanning. *TEACHING Exceptional Children, 33*(4), 24–30.

Individuals With Disabilities Education Improvement Act of 2004 (IDEA), 20 U.S.C. § 1400 *et seq.* (2004; reauthorization of the Individuals with Disabilities Education Act of 1990).

Johnson, D. W., Johnson, R. T., & Stanne, M. B. (2000). Cooperative learning methods: A meta-analysis. Retrieved August 1, 2005, from http://www.co-operation .org/pages/cl-methods.html

Levine, M. (2002). *A mind at a time.* New York: Simon and Schuster.

Magiera, K., Smith, C., Zigmond, N., & Gebauer, K. (2005). Benefits of co-teaching in secondary mathematics classes. *TEACHING Exceptional Children, 37*(3), 20–24.

Mastropieri, M. A., Scruggs, T. E., Graetz, J., Norland, J., Gardizi, W., & McDuffie, K. (2005). Case studies in co-teaching in the content areas: Successes, failures, and challenges. *Intervention in School and Clinic, 40*, 260–270.

Murawski, W. W. (2005). *Co-teaching in the inclusive classroom: Working together to help all your students find success.* Bellevue, WA: Bureau of Education and Research.

Murawski, W. W. (2006). Student outcomes in co-taught secondary English classes: How can we improve? *Reading and Writing Quarterly, 22*, 227–247.

Murawski, W. W., & Dieker, L. A. (2004). Tips and strategies for co-teaching at the secondary level. *TEACHING Exceptional Children, 36*(5), 52–58.

Murawski, W. W., & Lochner, W. W. (2007). *Co-teaching solutions system: Toolbox and observation system.* Shepherdstown, WV: Wide River Educational Consulting Company.

Murawski, W. W., & Swanson, H. L. (2001). A meta-analysis of co-teaching research: Where are the data? *Remedial and Special Education, 22*, 258–267.

No Child Left Behind Act of 2001, 20 U.S.C. 70 § 6301 et seq. (2002).

Rea, P. (2005). 20 ways to engage your administrator in your collaboration initiative. *Intervention in School and Clinic, 40*, 312–316.

Rea, P. J., McLaughlin, V. L., & Walther-Thomas, C. (2002). Outcomes for students with learning disabilities in inclusive and pull-out programs. *Exceptional Children, 72*, 203–222.

Scruggs, T. E., Mastropieri, M. A., & McDuffie, K. A. (2007). Co-teaching in inclusive classrooms: A metasynthesis of qualitative research. *Exceptional Children, 73*, 392–416.

Spencer, S. A. (2005). An interview with Dr. Lynne Cook and Dr. June Downing: The practicalities of collaboration in special education service delivery. *Intervention in School and Clinic, 40*, 296–300.

Stanford, P. (2003). Multiple intelligence in every classroom. *Intervention in School and Clinic, 39*, 80–85.

Struyk, L. R., Epstein, M. H., Bursuck, W., Polloway, E. A., McConeghy, J., & Cole, K. B. (1995). Homework, grading, and testing practices used by teachers for students with and without disabilities. *Clearing House, 69*(1), 50.

Thurlow, M. L. (2002). Positive educational results for all students: The promise of standards-based reform. *Remedial and Special Education, 23*, 195–202.

Tomlinson, C. A. (2005). *An educator's guide to differentiating instruction.* Boston: Houghton-Mifflin.

Walther-Thomas, C. S. (1997). Coteaching experiences: The benefits and problems that teachers and principals report over time. *Journal of Learning Disabilities, 30*, 395–407.

Weiss, M., & Lloyd, J. W. (2002). Congruence between roles and actions of secondary special educators in co-taught and special education settings. *The Journal of Special Education, 36*(2), 58–68.

Wilson, G. L. (2005). This doesn't look familiar! A supervisor's guide for observing co-teachers. *Intervention in School and Clinic, 40*, 271–275.

Originally published in *TEACHING Exceptional Children*, Vol. 40, No. 4, pp. 40–48.

3

Purposeful Assessment Practices for Co-Teachers

Greg Conderman and Laura Hedin

Stephanie and Eveard co-teach reading in their second-grade classroom. They think students are making progress on critical skills associated with district and state standards. Julia and Joe co-teach middle school mathematics. They are unsure how to group students instructionally and how to determine what students already know regarding an upcoming instructional unit. Myrna and Arlo co-teach high school science and rely on publisher-developed multiple-choice tests as their primary assessment tool. All of these co-teachers are involved in co-planning and co-instructing, but they are unsure how to approach co-assessment. Specifically, they have not yet established ways to capitalize on each other's assessment expertise, vary the type of assessment, or differentiate assessments based on students' individualized education programs (IEPs). Consequently, they hope students are making progress, rely on assessment practices they have used in the past, or provide the same assessment for all students. This article explores ways that co-teachers can collaboratively discuss, use, and differentiate assessments to inform instruction.

Friend and Cook (2010) defined *co-teaching* as "a service delivery option for providing special education or related services to students with disabilities or other special needs . . . in their general education classes" (p. 109). In co-taught classes, students with disabilities receive instruction from highly qualified teachers, interact with a rigorous curriculum, and receive necessary individualized supports and interventions as noted in their IEPs (Conderman & Hedin, 2010).

Co-teaching occurs as two professionals share responsibilities for all students within a common space and has three components: co-planning, co-instructing, and co-assessing (Conderman, Bresnahan, & Pedersen, 2009; Conderman & Hedin 2010; Dieker & Murawski, 2003; Murawski, 2008). There are various instructional models from which to choose (e.g., one teach/ one assist, one teach/one observe, station, parallel, alternative, and team teaching) to meet diverse student needs while differentiating instruction, thereby supporting students' progress toward general education standards. Each co-teaching model allows teachers to collaborate by differentiating instruction and assessments.

WHAT IS CO-ASSESSMENT?

To date, the professional co-teaching literature has emphasized co-planning (e.g., Bryant & Land, 1998; Murawski & Dieker, 2004; Ploessl, Rock, & Schoenfeld, 2010) and co-instructing (e.g., Rice, Drame, Owens, & Frattura, 2007; Wilson, 2008). Researchers have rarely investigated the ways teachers differentiate assessments and the effects of co-assessment in co-taught settings.

Magiera and Zigmond (2005) reported that special educators in co-taught classrooms frequently monitored students' progress during independent practice, however, they did not discuss subsequent teacher decision-making processes facilitated by this monitoring. Hang and Rabren (2009) conducted co-teaching surveys with teachers and students. The 31-item teacher survey included only two assessment-related items, and the 19-item student survey included only one. None of the classroom dimensions during co-teaching observations related to assessment. Similarly, Harbort and colleagues (2007) coded secondary co-teachers' classroom behaviors using momentary time sampling; however, none of the coding categories explicitly referred to assessment or evaluation of student performance.

Researchers also have observed that co-teachers tend to use the one teach/one assist model (Scruggs, Mastropieri, & McDuffie, 2007). Because this model may not allow co-teachers to purposefully use multiple opportunities to assess students' performance, adjust instruction based on data, or collaborate to strengthen and differentiate assessments, Murawski and Hughes (2009) recommended that co-teachers use the full range of co-teaching models and components, including co-assessment.

TYPES AND USES OF EDUCATIONAL ASSESSMENT

Assessment refers to the process of gathering data on student performance to inform instructional decision making (Nitko & Brookhart, 2010). Due to the range of information gleaned through assessments, no single measure provides sufficient information for a global picture of student progress (Nolet & McLaughlin, 2005). Teachers need to have available and base their decisions on data from various assessments, such as those described in Table 1. Table 1 illustrates how—based on their skills, familiarity with assessments, and relationship with students—co-teachers can share assessment responsibilities. Planning for *purposeful co-assessment* occurs at four points in time: as co-teaching teams form, before lessons or units of study begin, during instruction, and after instruction.

PURPOSEFUL ASSESSMENT BEFORE TEAMS BEGIN

When forming teaching partnerships, co-teachers should discuss their assessment philosophies, and practices and strategies for handling conflict. Discussing assessment and grading requirements, preferences, practices, progress-monitoring systems, and philosophies early in the co-teaching relationship may prevent later misunderstanding and conflict. Figure 1 includes questions that we developed and used with Illinois middle school co-teachers to guide this discussion.

Because co-teachers may or may not have similar assessment experiences, strengths, backgrounds, and philosophies, when sharing assessment skills and beliefs it is important to listen carefully and to consider ways to collaborate and build on each other's strengths. For example, while discussing questions from Figure 1, Myrna shared her experiences developing summative assessments, constructing rubrics, and using the school's reporting grading system; Arlo noted his expertise developing formative assessments, designing progress-monitoring systems, and modifying assessments—all of which can be used effectively in their co-taught classroom.

During this discussion, co-teachers may discover that some assessment practices may not represent personal choices or decisions but are constraints placed on them. For example, content-area teachers may have limited flexibility selecting assessments due to departmental and content-area standards. Similarly, students' IEPs may dictate timing assessment accommodations associated with presentation mode; response mode; and scheduling, setting, and linguistics (Salend, 2008).

During this phase, co-teachers should agree on how they will share responsibilities such as grading, developing rubrics and scoring sheets, maintaining the grade book, communicating student progress to parents, gathering data for response-to-intervention decisions, and ensuring that testing accommodations are prepared and implemented. In other words, they must determine how assessment practices in their classroom will be more effective with two professionals sharing tasks and how to differentiate between reporting of grades and ongoing assessment of learning activities. Co-assessment should result in more accurate and informative data than one teacher alone can collect. This assessment may involve evaluating student learning more frequently or through one-on-one situations rather than whole-group settings, providing more frequent and detailed feedback to students and parents, differentiating instruction based on assessment results, and differentiating

Table 1. Types of Assessments and Their Use

Type of Assessment	Use	Example in Co-Taught Classroom
Norm-referenced	To compare a student's score to others in the same age or grade	Together, Myrna and Arlo review student reading scores from recent state exams. They choose different leveled reading materials matched to student scores and decide which students need additional reading accommodations.
Criterion-referenced	To compare a student's score to a predetermined standard	Stephanie and Eveard require all students to earn at least 90% on their phonemic awareness test. Stephanie teaches the whole group; Eveard reassesses individual students.
Individual-referenced	To compare a student's score with his or her previous performance	Teri and Dave note individual student growth over time on written science lab reports. Teri reteaches writing skills to students demonstrating minimal gains.
Curriculum-based	To determine the student's knowledge of or skills with material presented in the curriculum	Violet and Les administer weekly math quizzes on skills covered during the week. They divide the grading, each scoring $\sim$ 14 quizzes on Fridays.
Performance-based	To provide opportunities for students to apply skills or knowledge to real-life situations which require problem-solving skills	Students in Maria and Toni's Basic Math class complete real-life problems and projects to demonstrate course competencies. Teachers share responsibility for developing projects.
Self-assessments	To encourage self-reflection and analysis	Students in Sal and Bonita's Composition 1 class set writing goals and reflect on their progress. Both teachers conduct weekly conferences with students.
Alternative	To provide a different method of gathering information about the progress of students who do not participate in state assessments	Greta, a seventh grader with intellectual disability, maintains a portfolio to demonstrate her progress in language arts. Her co-teachers help her organize materials for her upcoming student-led IEP conference.

Figure 1. Checklist for Purposeful Co-Assessment

Teaching partners: Subject area/course number:		Date: Semester:
Consideration	**Yes/No**	**Resources**
Before co-teaching teams begin, have we . . .		
Discussed our strengths and needs regarding assessment practices?	Y/N	Conderman, Bresnahan, & Pedersen (2009); McNair, Bhargava, Adams, Edgerton, & Kypros (2003)
Decided how to share grading responsibilities?	Y/N	Silva, Munk, & Bursuck (2005)
Planned how both teachers will be purposefully engaged during co-teaching?	Y/N	Friend & Cook (2010)
Discussed IEP assessment accommodations and modifications?	Y/N	Elliott & Thurlow (2006); Salend (2008)
Before instruction, have we . . .		
Collected relevant data on students' existing knowledge and skills?	Y/N	Conderman et al. (2009); Provost, Lambert, & Babkie (2010)
Created a system for monitoring students' assessment data?	Y/N	Garcia (2007); Lingo, Barton-Arwood, & Jolivette (2011)
Planned postinstruction assessments aligned with learning objectives?	Y/N	Honolulu Community College (2011)
Aligned co-teaching models with assessment practices?	Y/N	Friend & Cook (2010); Villa, Thousand, & Nevin (2004)
Planned for assessment activities that will activate students' background knowledge?	Y/N	Connor (2003); Ogle (1989)
During instruction, have we . . .		
Organized the classroom and instruction to facilitate ongoing assessment?	Y/N	Wadsworth & Knight (1999)
Planned opportunities for students to demonstrate their understanding through active engagement?	Y/N	Moss & Crowley (2011)
Determined how data on student responses will be collected and used?	Y/N	Stecker, Lembke, & Foegen (2008)
After instruction, have we . . .		
Conducted formative and summative assessments aligned with learning objectives?	Y/N	McMillan & Nash (2000)
Used different types of assessments and co-teaching formats aligned with lesson objectives and student characteristics?	Y/N	Conderman & Koroglanian (2002)
Followed IEP requirements for accommodations and modifications?	Y/N	Laitusis & Cook (2007); Salend (2008)

assessments. In short, co-assessment requires both teachers to assume active roles in planning, implementing, and evaluating assessments, differentiating their roles between reporting grades and assessing learning and behaviors. Teachers also should discuss assessments they will use before, during, and after instruction.

PURPOSEFUL ASSESSMENT BEFORE INSTRUCTION

Co-teachers may have several sources of student assessment data to use before instruction. Although no one way is the correct way to use available data, co-teachers should consider what data they have and how they can put it to best use.

Standardized Test Scores

Teachers typically have results of recent state or district tests. Co-teachers can review their class profile of standardized test scores to identify class strengths and needs and differentiate skill instruction for individuals and small groups. For example, middle school language arts co-teachers Joel and Marshall developed a spreadsheet with students' most recent standardized reading and writing scores. They color-coded scores indicating students at or above grade level (green), approaching grade level (yellow), or achieving below grade level (red). Color-coding provided a quick visual reference that they used to choose instructional materials and plan small-group instruction. Their spreadsheet also included students' assessment accommodations or modifications, serving as a helpful reminder during instruction and before administering classroom tests. Implementing accommodations before high-stakes tests allows teachers to determine whether accommodations are valid, effective, useful, and fair (Cox, Herner, Demczyk, & Nieberding, 2006); using accommodations for the first time on a high-stakes test may confuse or frustrate students (Laitusis & Cook, 2007).

Based on standardized test scores and other available data, Joel and Marshall designed five learning stations, and students rotated through four. At Centers 1 through 3, all students completed activities based on core language arts standards. The remaining two centers differentiated activities. For example, Center 4 included explicit instruction in paragraph writing using the TREE strategy (Harris, Graham, & Mason, 2002), and Center 5 included an advanced vocabulary activity. By differentiating instruction during station teaching, Joel and Marshall met individual needs based on available assessment data.

Curriculum-Based Assessments

Curriculum-based assessments (CBA) provide teachers with information on how well a student performs on materials or skills associated with a particular course. Typically, teachers transform books or curriculum materials into probes or quick informal assessments. Universal screening tools such as Aimsweb provide curriculum-based information about students' reading and math performance. Teachers can also print data reports available through progress-monitoring systems with published curricula. Data from these probes help co-teachers anticipate what students have already mastered or may find challenging in the curriculum.

First grade co-teachers Bethany and Danae used alternative teaching to deliver Tier 2 and 3 reading interventions. They used fall universal screening data to select students requiring Tier 2 interventions in addition to regular guided reading instruction. One teacher used explicit instruction for teaching letter sounds and sounding out regular consonant-vowel-consonant words with a small group while the other teacher conducted regular reading instruction with the remainder of the class. They frequently alternated roles, so both could get to know each student's individual needs, enhancing later discussion of observations and progress-monitoring data.

Additional Before-Instruction Assessments

Before an instructional unit, co-teachers can assess what students already know by using the What I Know (K) and What I Want to Know (W) columns of a KWL chart (Ogle, 1989), class discussions, pretests, or anticipation guides (a series of statements to which students respond prior to reading a selection; Connor, 2003). Co-teachers have more options for using these tools than if they taught by themselves. For example, elementary teachers Wanda and Heather often each lead discussion of the K and W steps with half the class (parallel teaching) to encourage more student participation. On other occasions, Wanda asks the large group probing questions about an upcoming unit while Heather gathers data regarding which students respond as well as the accuracy and quality of their statements (one teach/one observe).

Pretests or anticipation guides also serve as before-instruction assessments and can be used effectively in co-taught classrooms. Wanda and Heather can support students individually or in small groups by (a) using video, computer, and audio text supplements; (b) highlighting important statements; (c) allowing students to work with a partner or group; (d) allowing additional time for completion; and (e) adjusting the difficulty level through content, format, or reading level. Even with these adaptations, as much as possible, pretests and anticipation guides should be similar in length and print size as not to embarrass students (Kozen, Murray, & Windell, 2006).

Another group of CBA occurs as students enter the room. Warm-ups, admit slips, sponges, quick writes, or bell ringers—all of these are 2- to 5-minute activities that co-teachers can display on the overhead or write on the board and have students complete immediately upon entering the classroom, with the purpose of reviewing the previous day's lesson or gathering background knowledge before beginning a new lesson. Other assessments assess content knowledge or what students know. *Admit slips* are written responses to open-ended questions/statements used as quick writes prior to the beginning of the lesson such as *Write one (or more) things that you already know about* [topic] or *Write one question that you still have about the activity that we completed yesterday.* These brief assessments help co-teachers establish content for re-teaching, activate prior knowledge, and set a purpose for learning—practices that improve learning outcomes, particularly for students with disabilities (Carr & Thompson, 1996). Based on results of their bell-ringers, Wanda and Heather provided parallel teaching the following day. They divided the class into two heterogeneous groups to demonstrate a key concept prior to the main lesson. Discussing the demonstration in smaller groups allowed more students to express their thoughts and build their background knowledge in the same timeframe, and the teachers were better able to evaluate students' prior knowledge.

PURPOSEFUL ASSESSMENT DURING INSTRUCTION

During instruction, co-teachers can use numerous activities to determine whether their instruction is effective and whether students are acquiring critical skills or content. For example, during one teach/one assist, Arlo conducts ongoing on-the-spot "over-the-shoulder" student observations as Myrna leads instruction. Julia and Joe discovered that with parallel or station teaching, they could interact with students more closely, view written assignments, respond to student questions, and reteach as needed. As Scruggs et al. (2007) noted, students respond positively to co-taught classes in part because they have access to support when they need it.

In a co-taught classroom, not only can teachers respond to questions more promptly, but they also can meet students' needs by adjusting the prompt (i.e., type of question) and response mode (e.g., verbal versus written). For example, during a quiz, Arlo noticed that several students did not understand the wording on a problem. He verbally restated the question, which allowed students to successfully complete the problem. Based on additional observations, Myrna and Arlo decided to teach students about the different question types (Raphael & Au, 2005) that often appear on chapter and standardized tests.

ASSESSMENTS TO PROMOTE ENGAGEMENT

There are several ways co-teachers can promote active engagement to help students integrate new knowledge with background knowledge and construct new or revise existing understandings (Anderson, Wang, & Gaffney, 2006). For example, while reviewing phonemes, Stephanie and Eveard frequently ask questions for all students to respond in unison. Unison responses encourage all students to actively practice many skills throughout an instructional period, provide teachers with frequent information about each student's progress, maintain students' attention, and significantly accelerate student progress (Carnine, Silbert, Kame'enui, & Tarver, 2010).

Similarly, Julia and Joe often use dry-erase boards for students to display math responses. Many students are willing to use a dry-erase board rather than paper and pencil because of the ease with which they can change or erase their answers (Clare, 1996). Further, due to their flexibility, dry-erase boards can be used many times throughout a lesson (Clare, 1996) and replace worksheet or workbook materials, saving money and paper.

Students in Stephanie and Eveard's class like using response cards. They display the card that represents their self-assessed understanding of the lesson (i.e., red = stop, I'm lost; yellow = I need a little clarification; green = I understand everything). Students can also use the cards to indicate if a statement expressed by the teacher is true (green) or false (red). Response cards improve learners' classroom engagement, the amount they learn, and the amount they retain (Christle & Schuster, 2003). Further, some learners prefer response cards to hand-raising (Christle & Schuster, 2003). In all of these situations, the assisting co-teacher can observe and document student responses.

In classrooms with computer/projectors or interactive whiteboards, co-teachers can use clickers or personal response systems (PRS) to assess students' understanding during the lesson (Barnes, 2008). With PRS, teachers embed multiple-choice or true-false questions into the lesson PowerPoint using specialized computer software. When the question slide appears, students respond anonymously using their personal remote control unit (i.e., clicker). After all students have responded, the software generates a bar or line graph depicting the group's responses, which allows teachers to decide if they should advance to the next skill or reteach the concept. Kay, LeSage, and Knaack (2010) found that secondary students using PRS increased their level of engagement. Further, teachers effectively collected and used formative assessment data, which students appreciated.

PURPOSEFUL ASSESSMENT AFTER INSTRUCTION

Co-teachers can use formative or summative assessments after instruction. For example, student "exit slips" provide valuable formative data. One to 5 minutes prior to dismissal, students create an exit slip by writing a response to a teacher-created prompt such as: (a) summarize the main idea and one detail from (chapter just discussed); (b) list the four steps of (the water cycle, photosynthesis, finding the perimeter of a circle from its radius); or (c) write one thing your project group accomplished today, one question you have, and the next step your group will take. Additionally, students can reread their admit slip (written before instruction) and revise it; creating a "First I thought . . . Now I know . . ." response. Instructional systems, such as self-regulated strategy development (Harris, Santangelo, & Graham, 2008), that incorporate strategies along with goal-setting prior to instruction and specific feedback to students have produced large positive effects for students with disabilities. Together, co-teachers may have more opportunities to develop and assess student responses from admit and exit slips, provide specific feedback to students, and help students set and monitor individualized goals.

Summative Assessments

Co-teachers also can decide which summative assessments to use after instruction, such as portfolios, checklists, rating scales, products or projects evaluated with rubrics, quizzes, tests, and report-card grades. These assessments show the cumulative progress of a student over a defined unit of study or period of time. Having two professionals develop, discuss, and review these helps ensure that they reflect students' developmental levels, accommodations or modifications, and assessment best practices.

Assessing Student Products

Co-teachers can share portfolio responsibilities by conferencing with students individually or in small groups, helping students set reasonable goals and choose appropriate artifacts, following up with students who were absent or are not maintaining their portfolios, and helping students plan their student-led parent-teacher conference or IEP meeting. Alternate teaching provides one teacher an opportunity to conference with students while the other continues with the day's lesson.

In addition to portfolios, students can use rubrics, checklists, and rating scales as self-assessments to guide the preparation of their work. Co-teachers can differentiate these products by adjusting outcomes, simplifying wording, individualizing overall point totals and point emphasis, and providing examples and nonexamples. Some students may need these tools read or explained more thoroughly, which can occur more easily with two teachers. Further, co-teachers can team teach to model these and other self-assessments for the whole class.

Grading Student Products

Finally, co-teachers can collaborate when developing and grading projects, quizzes, and tests, and calculating final grades. Co-teachers can review projects, assignments, and assessments for appropriate reading and language levels, format, clarity of directions, difficulty level, and other best practices in test development such as rewriting multiple-choice questions as direct questions, placing fill-in-the-blanks at the end of sentences, limiting matching sections to no more than 10 items, and ensuring that true/false questions assess only one concept (Conderman & Koroglanian, 2002).

A student with a disability in co-taught classrooms may have an individualized grading system which bases part of his or her assignment or report-

card grade on progress toward IEP objectives, improvement over past performances, prioritized content and assignments, effort, and/or modified
weights and scales (Silva, Munk, & Bursuck, 2005). Both co-teachers must be
aware of how all students will be graded and reasons for changes in the grading system, which need to be discussed, agreed upon, and documented by
the IEP team and administrator.

FINAL THOUGHTS

Co-teaching provides opportunities for students with disabilities to interact
with a rigorous curriculum and receive quality instruction from two certified
teachers. However, for students to receive the maximum benefits of a co-
taught classroom and for co-teachers to maintain parity, both teachers must
be actively involved in co-planning, co-instructing, and co-assessing. Co-
assessing, a neglected component in the professional literature, provides a
unique opportunity for partners to discuss assessment and grading philosophies, share assessment responsibilities, and collaborate on ways to differentiate assessments. Special educators must be willing to share these
responsibilities and ensure that students with disabilities receive necessary
assessment accommodations and grading adaptations directed by their IEPs.
    After discussing their philosophy and approach to assessment, co-teach-
ers can identify the assessments they will use before, during, and after

instruction. Before-instruction assessments may include reviewing recent district or state test scores or gathering data from curriculum-based assessments, K-W-L charts, class discussions, pretests, or anticipation guides. During-instruction assessments may include on-the-spot (over-the shoulder) student checks, unison responses, whiteboards, response cards, or PRS; after-instruction assessments may include exit slips, projects, portfolios, self-assessments, homework, quizzes, tests, and report-card grades.

Regardless of the assessment, co-teachers who are deliberate and plan can ensure that their assessment practices utilize the skills and strengths of both teachers, are different and perhaps more frequent than if they were teaching a class on their own, reflect best practices in assessment, and most important, accurately assess what students have learned. These practices help co-teachers like Stephanie and Eveard, Julia and Joe, and Myrna and Arlo realize the promise and potential of co-assessing.

REFERENCES

Anderson, R. C., Wang, Q., & Gaffney, J. S. (2006). Comprehension research over the past three decades. In K. A. D. Stahl & M. C. McKenna (Eds.), *Reading research at work: Foundations of effective practice* (pp. 275–823). New York, NY: Guilford Press.

Barnes, L. J. (2008). Lecture-free high school biology using an audience response system. *American Biology Teacher, 70*, 531–536. http://dx.doi.org/10.1662/0002-685-70.9.531

Bryant, M., & Land, S. (1998). Co-planning is the key to successful co-teaching. *Middle School Journal, 29*(5), 28–34.

Carnine, D. W., Silbert, J., Kame'enui, E. J., & Tarver, S. G. (2010). *Direct instruction reading* (5th ed.). Boston, MA: Pearson-Merrill.

Carr, S. C., & Thompson, B. (1996). The effects of prior knowledge and schema activation strategies on the inferential reading comprehension of children with and without learning disabilities. *Learning Disability Quarterly, 19*(1), 48–61. http://dx.doi.org/10.2307/1511053

Christle, C. A., & Schuster, J. W. (2003). The effects of using response cards on student participation, academic achievement, and on-task behavior during whole-class math instruction. *Journal of Behavioral Education, 12*, 147–165. http://dx.doi.org/10.1023/A:1025577410113

Clare, S. M. (1996). Dry-erase boards for students' responses to classroom exercises. *Mathematics Teacher, 89*, 724.

Conderman, G., Bresnahan, V., & Pedersen, T. (2009). *Purposeful co-teaching: Real cases and effective strategies.* Thousand Oaks, CA: Corwin Press.

Conderman, G., & Hedin, L. (2010, September). *Co-teaching: Part 2.* Presentation at Downers Grove South High School, Downers Grove, IL.

Conderman, G., & Koroglanian, C. (2002). Writing test questions like a pro. *Intervention in School and Clinic, 38*(2), 83–87. http://dx.doi.org/10.1177/10534512020380020301

Connor, J. (2003, September). *Instructional reading strategy: Anticipation guides.* Retrieved from http://www.indiana.edu/ ~ l517/anticipation_guides.htm

Cox, M. L., Herner, J. G., Demczyk, M. J., & Nieberding, J. (2006). Provision of testing accommodations for students with disabilities on statewide assessments: Statistical links with participation and discipline ranks. *Remedial and Special Education, 27,* 346–354. http://dx.doi.org/10.1177/07419325060270060401

Dieker, L. A., & Murawski, W. W. (2003). Co-teaching at the secondary level: Unique issues, current trends, and suggestions for success. *The High School Journal, 86*(4), 1–13. http://dx.doi.org/10.1353/hsj.2003.0007

Elliott, J., & Thurlow, M. (2006). *Improving test performance of students with disabilities on district and state assessments.* Thousand Oaks, CA: Corwin Press.

Friend, M., & Cook, L. (2010). *Interactions: Collaboration skills for school professionals* (6th ed.). Upper Saddle River, NJ: Pearson.

Garcia, T. (2007). Facilitating the reading process. *TEACHING Exceptional Children, 39*(3), 12–17.

Hang, Q., & Rabren, K. (2009). An examination of co-teaching: Perspectives and efficacy indicators. *Remedial and Special Education, 30,* 259–268. http://dx.doi.org/10.1177/0741932508321018

Harbort, G., Gunter, P. L., Hull, K., Brown, Q., Venn, M. L., Wiley, L. P., & Wiley, E. W. (2007). Behavior of teachers in co-taught classes in a secondary school. *Teacher Education and Special Education, 30,* 13–23. http://dx.doi.org/10.1177/088840640703000102

Harris, K. R., Graham, S., & Mason, L. H. (2002). POW plus TREE equals powerful opinion essays. *TEACHING Exceptional Children, 34*(4), 70–73.

Harris, K. R., Santangelo, T., & Graham, S. (2008). Self-regulated strategy development in writing: Going beyond NLEs to a more balanced approach. *Instructional Science, 36,* 395–408. http://dx.doi.org/10.1007/s11251-008-9062-9

Honolulu Community College Faculty Development. (2011, January). *Teaching tips index: Assessment.* Retrieved from http://honolulu.hawaii.edu/intranet/committees/FacDevCom/guidebk/teachtip/teachtip.htm#assessment

Kay, R., LeSage, A, & Knaack, L. (2010). Examining the use of audience response systems in secondary school classrooms: A formative analysis. *Journal of Interactive Learning Research, 21,* 343–365.

Kozen, A., Murray, R., & Windell, I. (2006). Increasing all students' chance to achieve: Using and adapting anticipation guides with middle school learners. *Intervention in School and Clinic, 41,* 195–200. http://dx.doi.org/10.1177/10534512060410040101

Laitusis, C., & Cook, L. (2007). *Large-scale assessment and accommodations: What works?* Arlington, VA: Council for Exceptional Children.

Lingo, A., Barton-Arwood, S., & Jolivette, K. (2011). Teachers working together improving learning outcomes in the inclusive classroom: Practical strategies and examples. *TEACHING Exceptional Children, 43*(3), 6–13.

Magiera, K., & Zigmond, N. (2005). Co-teaching in middle school classrooms under routine conditions: Does the instructional experience differ for students with disabilities in co-taught and solo-taught classes? *Learning Disabilities Research and Practice, 20*(2), 79–85. http://dx.doi.org/10.1111/j.1540-5826.2005.00123.x

McMillan, J. H., & Nash, S. (2000, April). *Teacher classroom assessment and grading practices decision making.* Paper presented at the Annual Meeting of the National Council on Measurement in Education, New Orleans, LA. Retrieved from http://www.eric.ed.gov/PDFS/ED447195.pdf

McNair, S., Bhargava, A., Adams, L., Edgerton, S., & Kypros, B. (2003). Teachers speak out on assessment practices. *Early Childhood Education Journal, 31*(1), 23–31. http://dx.doi.org/10.1023/A:1025180617689

Moss, K., & Crowley, M. (2011). Effective learning in science: The use of personal response systems with a wide range of audiences. *Computers & Education, 56*(1), 36–43. http://dx.doi.org/10.1016/j.compedu.2010.03.021

Murawski, W. (2008, Nov.) *What is really happening in co-taught classrooms? One state knows!* Paper presented at the Annual Teacher Education Division Conference. Dallas, TX.

Murawski, W., & Dieker, L. (2004). Tips and strategies for co-teaching at the secondary level. *TEACHING Exceptional Children, 36*(5), 52–58.

Murawski, W., & Hughes, C. E. (2009). Response-to-intervention, collaboration, and co-teaching: A logical combination for successful systemic change. *Preventing School Failure, 53,* 267–277. http://dx.doi.org/10.3200/PSFL.53.4.267-277

Nitko, A., & Brookhart, S. (2010). *Educational assessment of students* (6th ed.). Des Moines, IA: Prentice Hall.

Nolet, V., & McLaughlin, M. (2005). *Accessing the general curriculum: Including students with disabilities in standards-based reform* (2nd ed.). Thousand Oaks, CA: Corwin Press.

Ogle, D. M. (1989). The know, want to know, learn strategy. In K. D. Muth (Ed.), *Children's comprehension of text: Research into practice* (pp. 205–223). Newark, DE: International Reading Association.

Ploessl, D. M., Rock, M. L., & Schoenfeld, N. (2010). On the same page: Practical techniques to enhance co-teaching interactions. *Intervention in School and Clinic, 45,* 158–168. http://dx.doi.org/10.1177/1053451209349529

Provost, M., Lambert, M., & Babkie, A. (2010). Informal reading inventories: Creating teacher-made literature based assessments. *Intervention in School and Clinic, 45,* 211–220. http://dx.doi.org/10.1177/1053451209353444

Raphael, T. E., & Au, K. H. (2005). QAR: Enhancing comprehension and test taking across grades and content areas. *The Reading Teacher, 59,* 206–221. http://dx.doi.org/10.1598/RT.59.3.1

Rice, N., Drame, E., Owens, L., & Frattura, E. M. (2007). Co-instructing at the secondary level: Strategies for success. *TEACHING Exceptional Children, 39*(6), 12–18.

Salend, S. (2008). Determining appropriate testing accommodations. *TEACHING Exceptional Children, 40*(4), 14–22.

Scruggs, T. E., Mastropieri, M. A., & McDuffie, K. A. (2007). Co-teaching in inclusive classrooms: A metasynthesis of qualitative research. *Exceptional Children, 73,* 392–416.

Silva, M., Munk, D., & Bursuck, W. (2005). Grading adaptations for students with disabilities. *Intervention in School and Clinic, 41*(2), 87–98. http://dx.doi.org/10.1177/10534512050410020901

Stecker, P. M., Lembke, E., & Foegen, A. (2008). Using progress-monitoring data to improve instructional decision making. *Preventing School Failure, 52,* 48–58. http://dx.doi.org/10.3200/PSFL.52.2.48-58

Villa, R. A., Thousand, J. S., & Nevin, A. I. (2004). *A guide to co-teaching: Practical tips for facilitating student learning* (2nd ed.). Thousand Oaks, CA: Corwin Press.

Wadsworth, D., & Knight, D. (1999). Preparing the inclusion classroom for students with special physical and health needs. *Intervention in School and Clinic, 34,* 170–175. http://dx.doi.org/10.1177/105345129903400309

Wilson, G. L. (2008). Be an active co-teacher. *Intervention in School and Clinic, 43,* 240–243. http://dx.doi.org/10.1177/1053451208314911

Originally published in *TEACHING Exceptional Children,* Vol. 44, No. 4, pp. 18–27.

4

Teachers Working Together: Improving Learning Outcomes in the Inclusive Classroom— Practical Strategies and Examples

Amy S. Lingo, Sally M. Barton-Arwood, and Kristine Jolivette

The Individuals With Disabilities Education Improvement Act (IDEA 2004), aligned with the No Child Left Behind Act (NCLB), emphasizes improved student academic outcomes. Because of these federal mandates, educators are required to monitor student progress and use that data to make instructional decisions. Historically, special education teachers working with students with disabilities have used data to measure progress toward goals and objectives in the students' individualized education programs (IEPs). However, with IDEA 2004, there is a "renewed emphasis on ensuring that children with disabilities are actually learning" (Pierangelo & Giuliani, 2006, p. 396), and that learning is connected to the general curriculum (IDEA 2004). With this focus on academic outcomes and access to the general curriculum, there is increased pressure for accountability in the education of students with disabilities in general education classrooms. Therefore, collaboration between general and special educators is more important than ever, as is a need for a variety of assessment strategies to support and document improved outcomes for students. There are multiple published resources available for educators that both describe various assessment strategies and tools as well as aid in their selection (e.g., examples of data collection forms; see Alberto & Troutman, 2006). However, educators also need concrete examples of how to incorporate these strategies into their collaborative classrooms to monitor daily instruction and how to make instructional decisions.

This article discusses seven options for data collection with classroom-based examples of how these assessment strategies can be used to facilitate improved academic outcomes for students. How can teachers collaborate on data collection and what are the implications for classroom use?

TEACHER COLLABORATION

Teacher collaboration has been defined broadly as "a style of direct interaction between at least two co-equal parties voluntarily engaged in shared decision making as they work toward a common goal" (Friend & Cook, 1992, p. 5). There are multiple methods of teacher collaboration, including co-teaching, peer coaching, collaboration consultation, and collaborative problem solving (Brownell, Adams, Sindelar, Waldron, & van Hover, 2006). Regardless of the model, the focus is on teachers working together with an assumption that collaboration leads to improved student academic achievement (Brownell et al., 2006; Scruggs, Mastropieri, & McDuffie, 2007; Zigmond & Magiera, 2002).

Measuring the success of collaboration in terms of student academic outcomes can be challenging. Although standardized achievement test data are readily available in most schools, those data do not always reflect immediate changes in student achievement. Therefore, teachers should consider more sensitive and detailed measures (Friend, 2007). For example, Marston (1996) compared reading progress of elementary students with mild disabilities served in inclusion-only, pull-out only, and combined service delivery models (i.e., co-teaching). Using curriculum-based measurement, the author reported that co-teaching was as effective as the resource room in producing reading gains. In a more recent example, Hunt, Soto, Maier, and Doering (2003) used interval recording to evaluate the collaborative team process (i.e., collaboration between general education teachers, special education teachers, and parents). Their outcomes indicated academic and social improvements in students with and at risk for disabilities in general education classrooms. These studies offer examples of successful teacher collaboration and the use of sensitive data collection methods to monitor and demonstrate student progress.

OPTIONS FOR MEASURING PROGRESS

Teachers of students with and without disabilities are required to monitor student progress. For students with disabilities, deficits in basic core content areas (e.g., reading and math) may limit access to the general curriculum and require teachers to plan instructional interventions to target deficiencies. With potential multiple areas of focus and instruction, it is crucial that teachers have useful methods to monitor the effectiveness of their instruction and to track student progress. A variety of data collection methods are available to general and special education teachers to support these monitoring and tracking activities. Educators may use anecdotal recording or permanent product recording. There also are methods based on a "numerical dimension of behavior" (Alberto & Troutman, 2006, p. 90) that include event recording (including frequency and rate), and interval recording (including partial, whole, and momentary time sampling). In addition, time-based data collection methods include duration and latency recording. Teachers may combine several methods to more efficiently and effectively monitor student behaviors (e.g., combine permanent product recording with event recording). Based on these data collection methods, the following examples of student academic behaviors are offered as practical examples of how teachers can work together to develop, interpret, and make instructional and intervention decisions based on assessment results in the classroom for the purpose of improving student outcomes. Examples of collaboration for each data collection method are provided in Table 1.

Although the data collection methods described in this article have been well-established in the literature for many years (e.g., Alberto & Troutman, 2006), some teachers may be hesitant to collect data. Teachers cited reasons such as not having enough time during the day to collect data or that data collection interferes with teaching (Alberto & Troutman, 2006). Although some data collection methods are more complex and less practical than others, general and special education teachers still have multiple options from which to choose depending on the types of academic behavior they need to assess. The following scenarios reflect realistic classroom situations and may help teachers realize the flexibility of data collection methods and the value in using data to inform instructional decisions.

TEACHER NOTES

Jamie is a third-grade student with reading difficulties. Her teacher, Mr. Vasquez, decides to use notes, also called anecdotal recording (Boyd-Batstone, 2004; Rhodes & Nathenson-Mejia, 1992) as an assessment tool. Anecdotal recording involves the narrative recording of events that occur during a specific period of time. Examples of this type of data collection include teacher notes written in a notebook, information written on Post-it notes, or home/school communication logs. After discussing this method with Ms. Lynch, the special education teacher, Mr. Vasquez decides he can easily use a notebook during guided reading instruction to record Jamie's errors (e.g., mispronounced words, skipped words, insertions, reversals), other reading variables (e.g., intonation, fluency, tone), and general observations (e.g., segments of instruction in which Jamie appears to have difficulty, comments Jamie makes about reading). The notes are written as observations in everyday language and do not interrupt the flow of instruction for Mr. Vasquez. From these anecdotal recordings, Mr. Vasquez and Ms. Lynch are able to ana-

Table 1. Examples of Collaboration for Data Collection of Academic Behaviors

Method and Description: Pros and Cons	Collection Tool and Data Analysis Example	Special Educator (SE) Role	General Educator (GE) Implementation	Intervention Example and Outcomes
Teacher Notes/ Anecdotal Recording: Narrative recording of events occurring during a specific time or setting • **Pros:** written in everyday language; can be collected during or after instruction • **Cons:** subjective information; challenging to summarize	• Teacher notes kept in a notebook • Teacher reads notes collected over time to identify recurring student error patterns (i.e., sight words, long pauses)	• Provides examples of anecdotal recording formats • Assists in observing and collecting anecdotal data and doing analysis • Recommends interventions • Provides follow-up consultation as needed	• Records data in notebook during guided reading • Shares data with SE • Implements interventions • Continues data collection to determine intervention effectiveness	• Student engages in sight word practice and listens to audiotaped models of fluent reading, then records and listens to self reading • Improved decoding, sight word identification and oral reading fluency
Student Work Sample and Permanent Product Recording: Concrete items resulting from student behavior • **Pros:** easy for all teachers; convenient; versatile; durable; does not require direct observation; minimal class disruption • **Cons:** none identified in literature	• Math multiplication worksheets • Examination of worksheets for specific error patterns	• Assists in defining behavior and appropriate permanent product methods (e.g., evaluates cursive writing using worksheets; evaluates public speaking using audiotape) • Provides data analysis • Recommends interventions	• Collects worksheets • Does error analysis with SE • Implements intervention • Monitors student progress (continues collecting and analyzing worksheets)	• Student participates in supplemental math program that provides additional practice on multiplication facts 6s, 7s, 8s, and 9s • Improved multiplication accuracy
Event Recording— Frequency: Number of times a behavior occurs during a specific, consistent time period • **Pros:** accurate for brief and discrete behavior; variety of data collection tools (e.g., paper/pencil, manual counter); minimal class disruption *continues*	• Paper numbered 1–10 with columns for weekly reading comprehension test. During weekly test, teacher records correct and incorrect student oral responses	• Provides information on differentiated instruction and formative evaluation • Develops model for data collection sheet	• Implements formative assessment procedures • Works with SE to evaluate data and determine next steps	• Instruction does not change, but student is allowed to participate in oral, versus written, assessment

continues

Table 1. *Continued*

Method and Description: Pros and Cons	Collection Tool and Data Analysis Example	Special Educator (SE) Role	General Educator (GE) Implementation	Intervention Example and Outcomes
Event Recording— Frequency - *continued* • **Cons:** not recommended for continuous, fast-paced behaviors lasting for extended periods of time				
Event Recording—Rate: Discrete behavior that can be observed in varying lengths of time • **Pros:** convenient; use for intervals for data collection • **Cons:** requires monitoring of length of time intervals and calculation of rate	• Math worksheet completed in 1 minute • Calculate the number of multiplication facts correct per minute	• Discusses student outcomes with GE • Problem-solves with GE; suggests expansion of data collection to monitor different aspects of behavior (i.e., fluency versus error analysis)	• Participates in reflection, data analysis, and intervention planning with SE	• Improved math accuracy and fluency
Interval Recording— Momentary Time Sampling: Number of intervals in which a behavior occurs, recorded at the end of an interval • **Pros:** student(s) only observed at the end of each interval; useful for continuous behaviors without clear beginning and ending; intervals typically consist of minutes, not seconds; can observe over extended periods of time and monitor more than one student • **Cons:** provides approximation, not actual number of times a behavior occurs; not recommended for infrequent behaviors	• Data collection sheet, numbered 1–15 to indicate 1-minute intervals; at the end of each minute, the teacher marks " + " if student is on-task and "–" if student is off task • Calculate the number and/or percentage of intervals student is on or off task	• Develops data collection sheet • Trains GE in how to use interval recording • Provides additional observations as needed • Problem-solves with GE to determine intervention to improve student on-task behavior	• Initiates discussion of student on-task behavior with SE • Collects data and problem-solves with SE • Implements intervention with SE support	• Whole class participates in an interdependent group contingency and earns reward for meeting criteria for on-task behavior • Classwide on-task behavior increases

continues

Table 1. *Continued*

Method and Description: Pros and Cons	Collection Tool and Data Analysis Example	Special Educator (SE) Role	General Educator (GE) Implementation	Intervention Example and Outcomes
Duration Recording: Recording the amount of time between the initiation of a response and its conclusion • **Pros:** exact measurement of how long the behavior occurs, the number of times the behavior occurs in a timeframe, calculate the average length of the time the behavior occurs, effective for low-frequency behaviors • **Cons:** time consuming and requires continuous observation of the student, may take time away from teaching	• Stop/start count-up digital timers • Determine the length of time to complete assigned task (e.g., complete lab report)	• Assists GE with setting up data collection system and data analysis • Meets with GE and student to determine improvement goals	• Uses timer to collect data • Meets with SE and student to determine improvement goals	• Goal setting with student to decrease amount of time needed to complete assignment
Latency Recording: Measurement of time between a prompt/stimulus and initiation of a task • **Pros:** exact measurement of time, average amount of time, effective data collection for low-frequency behaviors • **Cons:** time consuming and requires continuous observation of the student, may take time away from teaching	• Stop/start count-up digital timers • Record length of time between teacher request to start task and student beginning task	• Consults with GE to determine most efficient method to monitor academic problem • Collects and graphs data • Guides GE in setting and monitoring goals • Recommends additional instructional strategies to facilitate beginning academic tasks (e.g., modeling, guided practice)	• Facilitates classroom instruction while SE collects data • Works with SE to analyze data and determine time-based student goal • Implements targeted instructional strategies and monitors student performance	• Goal setting with student to decrease time between when teacher gives direction prompt to begin assignment and when student actually starts working on the assignment

Note: Adapted from Alberto & Troutman (2006); Kerr & Nelson (2006); Sulzer-Azaroff & Mayer (1991).

lyze Jamie's data in several ways to influence and plan future instruction (Rhodes & Nathenson-Mejia, 1992).

First, they identify an error pattern that includes a specific group of sight words that Jamie frequently mispronounces. Using this information, Ms. Lynch supports instruction in the classroom and engages Jamie in a brief warm-up at the beginning of reading to practice the previously missed sight words. During this review, Ms. Lynch provides Jamie with corrective feedback as well as reinforcement for increased accuracy. Mr. Vasquez also communicates with Ms. Lynch that he notices a pattern in his notes indicating that Jamie is experiencing fluency difficulties (e.g., long pauses between words and phrases). As a result, they provide Jamie with audiotapes of grade level passages that model fluent reading. Jamie listens to the tapes during flexible instructional time and then audiotapes herself reading the same passage. Over the next few weeks with log entries from both teachers, the anecdotal recordings indicate that Jamie has improved in sight word identification and reading fluency in grade level passages. Mr. Vasquez and Ms. Lynch reflect on their method of assessment; they were able to anecdotally record Jamie's reading performance using a nonintrusive method and use that data to make sound instructional decisions (i.e., more practice with sight words and fluency).

STUDENT WORK SAMPLES

In Mr. Fields's fourth-grade mathematics class, students complete weekly worksheets with multiplication facts for review and evaluation of this critical academic skill. Tameka is one of Mr. Fields's students with a mathematic disability; she frequently scores within the failing range on these worksheets. Typically, Mr. Fields collects the worksheets (i.e., the permanent product of student work; e.g., Jolivette, Wehby, Canale, & Massey, 2001) and simply scores the students' worksheets in terms of attempted and correct responses. During a collaborative conference, Mr. Grey, the special education teacher, suggests to Mr. Fields that in addition to identifying the number of problems completed correctly he could also conduct an error analyses; Mr. Grey then demonstrates how to identify error patterns. First, Tameka appears to correctly respond to certain fact families (0s, 1s, 2s, 3s, 4s, and 5s); however, she exhibits a high number of errors with the 6s, 7s, 8s, and 9s. Based on this data and his discussion with Mr. Grey, Mr. Fields decides to use a supplemental math intervention program that focuses on improving the accuracy of multiplication math facts, targeting the facts that are the most challenging for Tameka. Following this intervention, Tameka's scores have consistently improved each week, and an examination of Tameka's worksheets indicates that she is improving her accuracy on the 6s, 7s, 8s, and 9s.

EVENT RECORDING: FREQUENCY AND RATE

Event Example 1: Frequency

Maggie is a preservice teacher who is completing her student teaching in Mrs. Calhoun's second-grade inclusive classroom. Maggie has high expectations for all of the students, and as taught in her university classes, she collects and uses data on student achievement to inform her instructional decisions. When reviewing student scores on the weekly 10-question reading comprehension test, Maggie discovers that Robert, a student with Asperger's syndrome, is consistently only answering two to three questions correct per week. She is surprised by this information, as Robert is able to orally answer comprehension questions during class instruction and activities. During her planning period with Mrs. Calhoun, Maggie discusses the data and her concerns. Mrs. Calhoun has invited Ms. Paulsen, the special education teacher to participate.

As a result of their discussion, Ms. Paulsen provides Maggie with information on differentiated instruction. Maggie learns that differentiated instruction is a way for teachers to maximize academic success for each student by planning instruction that considers a student's individual needs and incorporates student interests and strengths (Tomlinson, 2006). As Maggie reflects about Robert's performance, she considers the fact that writing is difficult for him. She decides that giving Robert a written reading comprehension test is not really a valid method for evaluating his knowledge. Based on the information she has received about differentiated instruction, Maggie decides to provide Robert with the option to take an oral test. As suggested by Ms. Paulsen, Maggie uses event recording (e.g., Hitchcock, Prater, & Dowrick, 2004) to collect data on the accuracy of Robert's responses. Maggie makes a simple data sheet, numbered 1 to 10, and as Robert orally answers each question, Maggie easily marks a plus or a minus to document the frequency of correct and incorrect answers. Maggie quickly finds that Robert indeed has better comprehension than the written tests were indicating. He has consistently received scores of 10 out of 10 questions correct.

Event Example 2: Rate

In a previous example, Mr. Fields and Mr. Grey were using permanent product data to improve Tameka's accuracy on her mathematics multiplication worksheet. Both teachers and Tameka are pleased that her accuracy has improved, but Mr. Fields continues to monitor Tameka's progress in his class. One area that remains a concern is the amount of time it takes Tameka to complete the multiplication fact worksheets—about twice as long as her peers. Mr. Fields and Mr. Grey decide to take a more accurate measurement of Tameka's fluency rate as compared to a normed standard (i.e., peers within the school system). Tameka is given a "mad-minute" multiplication sheet and instructed to complete as many problems as she can within 1 minute. Mr. Grey then records rate in terms of the number of problems correct per minute (e.g., Jolivette, Lingo, Houchins, Barton-Arwood, & Shippen, 2006) and compares her rate to the fluency levels for her age. He finds that indeed her fluency rate is substantially lower than her peers. In response to this information, Mr. Grey and Mr. Fields discuss how to increase Tameka's multiplication fluency. They decide to pair Tameka with a peer. The two students take turns "coaching" each other in multiplication facts and then challenging each other to see how many problems each can answer in a minute. Mr. Grey continues to give Tameka the mad-minute worksheets twice a week. In reviewing the problems correct per minute over time, they find that Tameka has not only continued to improve in the accuracy of her multiplication facts, but she is performing at a faster rate, indicating improved skill fluency.

INTERVAL RECORDING: MOMENTARY TIME SAMPLING

Ms. Walls, a fifth-grade teacher, and Ms. Duke, a special education teacher, collaborate daily during reading instruction. Ms. Duke conducts individual reading checks, while Ms. Walls facilitates independent seatwork during the first 15 minutes of the school day. Ms. Walls informs Ms. Duke that many students are not completing their independent work, which is resulting in low grades. The teachers decide to initiate a system to reinforce students for staying on task (i.e., engaged in their independent work). Ms. Duke knows that using interval recording is an efficient method to determine the extent of student on task behavior (Jolivette et al., 2001). However, she knows that she and Ms. Walls will need to use a system where they can continue providing and monitoring instruction while collecting data. They decide to use a momentary time sampling system where they break the 15-minute period into shorter intervals (i.e., 1 minute). For a daily data sheet, Ms. Duke numbers a piece of paper from 1 to 15 to indicate 1-minute intervals. Instead of having to observe the entire interval, with momentary time sampling, the teachers simply look around the class at the end of each interval and record a plus when the whole class is on task or a minus when there are students off task (i.e., the whole class is not on task).

After 3 days of collecting data, the teachers calculate the number of intervals each day that the whole class was on task. The class was on task for 7 of the 15 intervals (47%) for the first day and 6 of the 15 intervals (40%) for the second and third days. Ms. Walls and Ms. Duke decide to implement an interdependent group reinforcement contingency (Alberto & Troutman, 2006). If all students are on task during at least 87% of the intervals (i.e., 13 out of 15 intervals) during the period, Ms. Walls places a marble in a jar. The jar is large enough to hold 20 marbles. When the marble jar becomes full, the students will receive an extra 15 minutes of free discussions on a topic of choice related to specific instructional goals (e.g., current events, upcoming school activity) at the end of the day. The students fill the jar at the end of a month. During a planning conference, Ms. Walls and Ms. Duke discover that during that month, students had completed more assignments, and their grades had improved as well.

DURATION RECORDING

Rebecca is a sophomore in Mr. Lang's chemistry class and does well on exams. However, she seldom turns in or completes her lab reports even though class time is provided to complete this task. As a result, she earned a failing grade for chemistry in the last grading period. After consulting with Ms. Charles, the special education teacher, the teachers decide to use duration recording (e.g., Kamps, Kravits, Stolze, & Swaggart, 1999) to find out how long it takes Rebecca to write her lab report. Ms. Charles suggests that Mr. Lang simply use a count-up timer and record the amount of time that Rebecca spends writing her lab results. Mr. Lang starts the timer when the class is to begin writing the lab report and stops the timer when Rebecca is either finished or the class is over. After recording duration on 3 separate days, Mr. Lang shows the data to Ms. Charles. The data showed that, across the 3 days, Rebecca spends an average of 35 minutes each class period writing her lab results. The teachers meet with Rebecca, and they all agree that her goal should be to spend no more than 20 minutes completing the lab write-up. After receiving this feedback, Rebecca becomes more aware of the amount of time she spends on her lab assignment and begins to complete her work more quickly. They know that Rebecca is doing better because Mr. Lang continues to collect duration data for a few weeks. He has commented to Ms. Charles that taking this type of data does not distract from his teaching. Ms. Charles also suggests that Mr. Lang provide Rebecca with a timer so she can monitor her own behavior during class.

LATENCY RECORDING

Luke often delays beginning academic tasks by displaying behaviors such as breaking his pencil lead, asking to see the counselor, or organizing his desk.

When Luke finally does begin the task, he often has many questions and claims not to understand the assignment. As a result, Luke rarely begins assignments when his peers do, and consequently does not finish assignments within the allotted time periods. Mr. Cook, Luke's general education teacher, and Ms. Crane, Luke's special education teacher, would like to see Luke begin assignments immediately so that he will have time to accurately complete his work. They decide that latency data could help them determine how quickly Luke begins his assignments (e.g., Wehby & Hollahan, 2000). When Mr. Cook gives directions for the class to begin the assignment, Ms. Crane begins to record the amount of time it takes for Luke to actually begin the assignment. After several days of recording this latency data, Ms. Crane and Mr. Cook tell Luke that it takes him an average of 8 1/2 minutes to begin his assignments. The teachers and Luke set a goal that he will begin the assignment within 3 minutes after the direction prompt is given. To ensure that Luke understands the assignment, Mr. Cook also begins to incorporate modeling and guided practice with the class before he asks them to begin assignments independently. Ms. Crane collects and graphs latency data daily to provide feedback to Luke regarding his progress in meeting the goal. After looking at the graph, the teachers clearly see that Luke is beginning his work in a more timely fashion. Although Luke has not yet met the 3-minute goal, he is clearly making progress as the time between the direction/prompt and beginning his work is decreasing daily. Mr. Cook decides not to make any instructional changes at this time and to continue to monitor Luke's progress. However, in addition to latency data, Ms. Crane also uses permanent product data (i.e., keeping and examining Luke's work) to monitor the number of assignments completed as well as the accuracy of his work.

CONCLUSION AND IMPLICATIONS FOR TEACHERS

The previous classroom-based examples highlight how general and special education teachers can work together and effectively and efficiently use various data collection methods in promoting improved student academic outcomes. With the increased emphasis of using data to make instructional decisions in the classroom, educators need to have the knowledge to select and use data collection methods appropriately in their classrooms. Practical data collection methods that can be incorporated into the daily flow of classroom activities are essential if educators are to engage in effective data collection to improve student educational outcomes.

The six data collection methods and examples for how to use each method within the context of a school or classroom setting are only a sampling of the many potential uses for the data collection methods showcased. Educators can take these examples and use or adapt them to meet the specific needs of their classes or individual students. For example, as suggested in the momentary time sampling example, teachers can use this method to collect data on an entire class. However, this method can also be used with

Table 2. Collaboration Steps to Measure Student Progress

Collaboration Steps	Considerations
1. Define student behavior to be monitored	Clearly defined behaviors are easier to measure.
2. Determine method for measuring progress	Consider the best method to minimize classroom disruptions.
3. Locate or design data collection form	Many data collection forms can be found online.
4. Determine roles	Decide who will collect data and when the data will be collected.
5. Collect data	Consider how much data or how long to collect data to accurately reflect student performance.
6. Analyze data	Putting data in a graph helps to more clearly see if students are actually making progress.
7. Determine next steps	Decide if an intervention is actually needed. Continue monitoring student progress.

small groups or individual students. Because time sampling relies only on a brief observation at the end of each interval, this method supports the use of direct observation data collection while teaching (Alberto & Troutman, 2006). In another example, Mr. Lang and Ms. Charles collected duration data and considered the possibility of teaching the student, Rebecca, to self-monitor (i.e., also collect duration data). Student self-monitoring provides an additional source of data and has been associated with increases in academic functioning (Harris, Friedlander, Saddler, Frizzelle, & Graham, 2005). In a third example, Ms. Crane, the special education teacher, helped collect latency data while working in Mr. Cook's classroom. When teachers work together, they can identify certain required tasks, such as teaching and data collection, and then divide the responsibilities. These classroom-based scenarios show how teachers can work together to evaluate the data and collaboratively use that data to make instructional decisions. See Table 2 for a summary of the steps involved in collaborating to measure student progress.

For specific examples of data collection sheets and graphs of data, readers are encouraged to use existing literature that provides excellent examples (for example, see Alberto & Troutman, 2006; Kerr & Nelson, 2006). Data collection may seem like a daunting task in light of all of the other tasks required of teachers. However, with good resources and supportive, collaborative

teaching relationships, data collection can be used to document student academic outcomes in response to classroom instruction and intervention.

REFERENCES

Alberto, P. A., & Troutman, A. C. (2006). *Applied behavior analysis for teachers* (7th ed.). Upper Saddle River, NJ: Merrill/Prentice-Hall.

Boyd-Batstone, P. (2004). Focused anecdotal records assessment: A tool for standards-based authentic assessment. *The Reading Teacher, 58,* 230–239.

Brownell, M. T., Adams, A., Sindelar, P., Waldron, N., & van Hover, S. (2006). Learning from collaboration: The role of teacher qualities. *Exceptional Children, 72,* 169–186.

Friend, M. (2007). The coteaching partnership. *Educational Leadership, 64*(5), 48–52.

Friend, M., & Cook, L. (1992). *Interactions: Collaboration skills for school professionals*. White Plains, NY: Longman.

Harris, K., Friedlander, B. D., Saddler, B., Frizzelle, R., & Graham, S. (2005). Self-monitoring of attention versus self-monitoring of academic performance: Effects among students with ADHD in the general education classroom. *The Journal of Special Education, 39*(3), 145–157.

Hitchcock, C. H., Prater, M. A., & Dowrick, P. W. (2004). Reading comprehension and fluency: Examining the effects of tutoring and video self-monitoring on first-grade students with reading difficulties. *Learning Disabilities Quarterly, 27*(2), 89–104.

Hunt, P., Soto, G., Maier, J., & Doering, K. (2003). Collaborative teaming to support students at risk and students with severe disabilities in general education classrooms. *Exceptional Children, 69*, 315–333.

Individuals With Disabilities Education Improvement Act of 2004 (IDEA 2004), 20 U.S.C. §§ 1400 et seq.

Jolivette, K., Lingo, A., Houchins, D. E., Barton-Arwood, S., & Shippen, M. E. (2006). Building math fluency for students with developmental disabilities and attentional difficulties using Great Leaps Math. *Education and Training in Developmental Disabilities, 41*, 392–400.

Jolivette, K., Wehby, J. H., Canale, J., & Massey, N. G. (2001). Effects of choice-making opportunities on the behavior of students with emotional and behavioral disorders. *Behavioral Disorders, 26*(2), 131–146.

Kamps, D., Kravits, T., Stolze, J., & Swaggart, B. (1999). Prevention strategies for at-risk students and students with EBD in urban elementary schools. *Journal of Emotional and Behavioral Disorders, 7*(3), 178–189.

Kerr, M. M., & Nelson, C. M. (2006). *Strategies for addressing behavior problems in the classroom* (5th ed.). Upper Saddle River, NJ: Merrill/Prentice-Hall.

Marston, D. (1996). A comparison of inclusion only, pull-out only, and combined service models for students with mild disabilities. *Journal of Special Education, 30*, 121–132.

The No Child Left Behind Act of 2001. 20 U.S.C. 70 § 6301 et seq. (2002).

Pierangelo, R., & Giuliani, G. A. (2006). *Assessment in special education: A practical approach* (2nd ed.). Boston, MA: Allyn & Bacon.

Rhodes, L. K., & Nathenson-Mejia, S. (1992). Anecdotal records: A powerful tool for ongoing literacy assessment. *The Reading Teacher, 45*, 502–509.

Scruggs, T. E., Mastropieri, M. A., & McDuffie, K. A. (2007). Co-teaching in inclusive classrooms: A metasynthesis of qualitative research. *Exceptional Children, 73*, 392–416.

Sulzer-Azaroff, B., & Mayer, G. R. (1991). *Behavior analysis for lasting change.* Fort Worth, TX: Holt, Rinehart, & Winston.

Tomlinson, C. A. (2006). Differentiating instruction for academic diversity. In J. M. Cooper (Ed.), *Classroom teaching skills* (pp. 151–184). Boston, MA: Houghton Mifflin.

Wehby, J. H., & Hollahan, S. M. (2000). Effects of high-probability requests on the latency to initiate academic tasks. *Journal of Applied Behavior Analysis, 33*(2), 259–262.

Zigmond, N., & Magiera, K. (2002). Co-teaching. *Current Practice Alerts, 6*, 1–4.

Originally published in *TEACHING Exceptional Children*, Vol. 43, No. 3, pp. 6-13.

5

Creating Optimal Opportunities to Learn Mathematics: Blending Co-Teaching Structures With Research-Based Practices

Jane M. Sileo and Delinda van Garderen

Ms. Thomas, the general educator, and Ms. Merced, the special education teacher, plan to co-teach mathematics classes during the upcoming school year. Based on previous interactions with students and knowledge of students' abilities from school records, they know that several students, including students with disabilities, struggle with mathematics (e.g., communication, problem solving, computation, and recalling facts, among other areas). Ms. Thomas and Ms. Merced also realize it is imperative to design lessons and activities in which all students have equal opportunities to develop mathematical knowledge and understanding. They discuss instructional content and methodology. Their biggest concern is how to create an effective learning environment. The teachers are familiar with co-teaching structures, but they believe it is important to use instructional strategies and practices that are effective for students with learning disabilities. The question is how to integrate the two practices. Throughout this article, we provide examples to demonstrate how Ms. Thomas and Ms. Merced integrated co-teaching and research-based mathematics strategies in their instruction.

As a result of the No Child Left Behind Act (NCLB, 2001) and Individuals With Disabilities Education Improvement Act (IDEA 2004), the U.S. Department of Education (2006) estimated that 48.9% of students with disabilities are educated in general classroom settings. Yet, many of these students struggle academically in various subject areas, including mathematics. Furthermore, approximately 5% to 8% of students experience learning disabilities in mathematics (Geary, 2004). Therefore, general and special educators need effective instructional strategies and service delivery models to meet the needs of all students.

A major expectation of teachers is their use of research-based instructional practices to teach mathematics (e.g., IDEA 2004; NCLB, 2001). Moreover, education literature includes many of these practices (e.g., strategy instruction) as well as instructional delivery models and structures (e.g., cooperative learning, co-teaching, and peer-tutoring) that are effective with students who have disabilities (Friend & Reising, 1993; Gately & Gately, 2001; Kroesbergen & van Luit, 2003; Montague & van Garderen, 2008; Pearl & Miller, 2007; van Garderen, Scheuermann, Jackson, & Hampton, 2009). However, the majority of research focuses exclusively on either instructional practices in mathematics or educational delivery models, such as co-teaching structures. Yet, the emphasis in education is to ensure that all students learn. Therefore, it is important to create optimal learning opportunities for everyone. The combination of research-based instructional practices in mathematics and co-teaching models may create powerful learning environments that enable all students to develop mathematical understandings.

WHAT IS CO-TEACHING?

Co-teaching is an instructional delivery model applicable to teaching students with disabilities in least restrictive integrated classroom settings in which general and special educators share responsibility for planning, delivering, and evaluating instructional practices for all students (Argüelles, Hughes, & Schumm, 2000; Villa, Thousand, & Nevin, 2008). Co-teaching allows teachers the opportunity to share expertise. General educators have knowledge of the curriculum, whereas special educators have knowledge of instructional processes for students who learn atypically (Ripley, 1997). In other words, "the expertise of the *masters of content*—the content area teachers—are blended with and supported by the expertise of the *masters of access*—the specialists in differentiating instruction" (Villa et al., p. 16). The greatest promise of co-teaching is the teachers' ability to provide academic and behavioral support for all students. It benefits (a) students with disabilities (e.g., improved academic performance, self-esteem, confidence, skills, and peer relationships); (b) students at risk of educational failure and others without disabilities with increased instructional time and individualized attention; and, (c) teachers with professional collaboration, satisfaction, and growth (Fontana, 2005; Jang, 2006; Kohler-Evans, 2006; Pearl & Miller, 2007; Villa et al.; Walther-Thomas, 1997).

BLENDING CO-TEACHING STRUCTURES WITH RESEARCH-BASED INSTRUCTION

According to Friend (2005), there are six basic co-teaching structures— (a) one teach, one observe, (b) team-teaching, (c) alternative teaching, (d) parallel teaching, (e) station teaching, and, (f) one teach, one drift—each of which may be modified depending on the academic subject and students' needs (Cook & Friend, 1995). These co-teaching structures blend nicely with selected research-based mathematics instructional practices that are appropriate for students who struggle with or have a disability in mathematics. The following discussion illustrates the application of mathematics instructional strategies and co-teaching structures in general education classrooms.

One Teach, One Observe

One teach, one observe occurs when one teacher teaches the whole group, and the other teacher observes the students (Cook & Friend, 1995). Because this was a new co-teaching relationship, Ms. Thomas and Ms. Merced decided that one teach, one observe was an excellent strategy to implement during the first few weeks of school. In one lesson, Ms. Thomas led a whole-class discussion about how to solve multistep addition computation problems. Ms. Merced observed students to determine who contributed to the discussion and then recorded the children's comments. The teachers paid particular attention to who was and who was not contributing to the discussion, as many students with disabilities have difficulty communicating what they are doing and learning, thus hindering their mathematical understanding (Baxter, Woodward, & Olson, 2005). Ms. Thomas and Ms. Merced used the process to determine which students needed extra encouragement and support to contribute to class discussions. As a way to promote dialogue, they provided students with question prompts, such as "What is the same or different about . . .," "Can you give an example from your own experience?," "Show me . . . tell me . . .," and, "If this is an answer, what might be the question?" (Watson, 2002).

During the school year, the teachers continued to use one teach, one observe to collect student data, monitor and support student behavior, and write and evaluate students' individualized education program (IEP) objectives in preparation for meetings with parents and colleagues. For example, Ms. Thomas noticed that a few students had difficulty attending to instruction during one lesson. As a result, she and Ms. Merced were concerned that these students were missing important information, which resulted in gaps in their knowledge base. With this information, Ms. Thomas and Ms. Merced set up a system where students would self-monitor their behavior and note when they were and were not paying attention (Salend, 2008). In addition to self-monitoring, one teacher periodically observed students to determine the amount of time they spent on the task.

Team Teaching

Team teaching occurs when the teachers share equally in planning and delivering all components of academic instruction. In team teaching, both teachers typically teach a large group of students either by standing side-by-side in front of a class or when they jigsaw instruction. According to Silberman (1996), jigsaw instruction occurs when teachers break down new material into manageable segments to facilitate students' learning, and where students subsequently teach the newly mastered material to their classmates. In this manner "each student learns something which, when combined with the material learned by others, forms a coherent body of knowledge or skill" (p. 111). This type of team teaching is similar to two general education teachers who work side-by-side, however in a co-teaching setting, the student–teacher ratio is smaller and the teachers blend their expertise (Friend & Cook, 2006).

In September, Ms. Thomas and Ms. Merced were teaching a number and operations unit, which focused on the whole number operations of addition and subtraction. The unit addressed contextualized problem types, which included various situations such as "change" problems where a beginning amount is altered to get an ending amount that is more or less (e.g., 26 pieces of fruit, 6 are eaten, leaving 20 pieces of fruit); "group" problems where smaller groups or parts combine to form a larger group (e.g., 8 dogs and 6 cats grouped together equal 14 pets); and "compare" problems where a larger amount, smaller amount, or difference is determined by comparing two amounts (e.g., Sue had 6 dolls and Lucy had 9 dolls, Lucy had 3 more dolls than Sue; Jitendra, 2002). Observation of several students, including those with disabilities, when solving word problems revealed their tendency to "grab" all the numbers and to add or subtract rather than stopping to understand the operations necessary to solve the problem. Ms. Merced researched the literature to identify strategies that help students to understand mathematical concepts underlying contextualized problems and to solve the problems. Based on research, she and Ms. Thomas decided to use Schema-Based Strategy Instruction in conjunction with team teaching because it promotes both conceptual understanding of, as well as a strategy for, solving word problems (Jitendra; Xin & Jitendra, 2006). The teachers believed this approach would benefit all students, not only those with difficulty solving contextualized problems. In addition, this structure helped the teachers support each other as they presented the material to ensure they addressed all steps and accurately reinforced the mathematical concepts.

Alternative Teaching

Alternative teaching occurs when one teacher teaches a small group of three to eight students while the other teaches the whole class (Cook & Friend, 1995). Alternative teaching is an excellent format to provide students with more intense and individualized instruction in a specific academic area.

As the school year progressed, Ms. Merced, the special education teacher, was concerned with the difficulty several students (both with and without disabilities) continued to incur when solving word problems. Therefore, to better understand their difficulties, she assessed them by requiring students to think-out-loud while solving the word problems and by asking them questions such as, "How did you solve this problem?" after they solved it. Assessment results highlighted students' need for further support and help to acquire and apply cognitive (e.g., visualization, paraphrasing, and estimation) and meta-cognitive (e.g., self-checking, self-monitoring, and self-questioning) processes and strategies that underlie effective and efficient problem solving (Montague, Warger, & Morgan, 2000). Based on these results, the teachers decided Ms. Merced would provide the students with explicit instruction on solving word problems twice weekly for approximately 15 to 20 minutes per session. This instruction would occur while Ms. Thomas worked on other word problem-solving activities with the remaining students in the class. Ms. Merced used the *Solve It!* program (Montague et al., 2000) to guide instruction and to teach students a step-by-step strategy that incorporates cognitive and meta-cognitive strategies for solving word problems.

Parallel Teaching

Parallel teaching occurs when teachers plan collaboratively and simultaneously teach the same academic content to two student groups (Friend, 2005). In parallel teaching, the class is often divided into two equal groups, and the teachers teach the same curriculum at the same time to a small group of students. Parallel teaching may be used in many different ways. However, the strength of the format is that it enables teachers to work with smaller numbers of students and to provide all students, but especially those with disabilities, an opportunity for individualized and hands-on learning.

Both Ms. Thomas and Ms. Merced recognized that use of various representational forms such as manipulative objects, diagrams and visual displays, and written symbols is an important part of developing students' mathematical understanding (Pape & Tchoshanov, 2001). Ms. Merced also knew that several studies demonstrated successful use of concrete-representational–abstract (CRA) instructional processes to teach numerous mathematical concepts and skills (e.g., algebra, multiplication, coin sums, place value, and geometry) to students with disabilities (Cass, Cates, Smith, & Jackson, 2003; Miller, Harris, Strawser, Jones, & Mercer, 1998; Miller, Mercer, & Dillon, 1992; Witzel, Smith, & Brownell, 2001). Although research has identified CRA as a successful instructional process, both teachers found it daunting to use manipulatives with a large group of students and to monitor student progress concurrently to ensure students' understanding of their new learning.

In February, Ms. Thomas and Ms. Merced taught a geometry unit that focused on the concepts of perimeter and area, in which they used the parallel teaching structure and CRA instructional process. Ms. Thomas and Ms.

Merced divided the class into two groups, moved the desks accordingly, and taught the same set of lessons to each group. This structure enabled them to utilize a more hands-on instructional approach, which, in turn, reduced potential problems using manipulative materials with a large group of students. More important, however, it allowed students to receive supplementary individualized instruction.

Station Teaching

According to Friend (2005), station teaching occurs when teachers divide responsibility for instructional content. In station teaching, teachers typically divide the class into groups with each group working on a different activity that contributes to attainment of one or more learning goals for all students (e.g., recalling multiplication facts 0 to 81).

As the year progressed, Ms. Merced and Ms. Thomas noticed a number of students still had difficulty recalling basic facts when working on complex mathematics problems. Ms. Merced identified several instructional practices that help students, particularly those with disabilities, to learn and recall basic facts. She and Ms. Thomas discussed the instructional practices and decided that the station teaching structure was an excellent format in which to practice and review math facts. In March, they decided that student groups would work at one station for approximately 5 to 10 minutes three times weekly at the beginning of each mathematics lesson. At the beginning of the next lesson, students rotated to another station, and so on. At each station, Ms. Thomas and Ms. Merced used a research-based instructional practice that helped students to practice and, in turn, reinforce their retention of multiplication facts.

At station one, students worked on their own where they used the Cover, Copy, Compare technique (McLaughlin & Skinner, 1996; Skinner, Ford, & Yunker, 1991). Here, students were presented an arithmetic fact (e.g., $3 \times 4 = 12$) that they look at, cover, and write an equation for, and then compare their written equation to the original example. If the written response matches the sample, students then move on to the next fact (Skinner et al.). In station two, the students used a visual mnemonic technique (Wood, Frank, & Wacker, 1998) that relied on flash cards containing a math fact with a picture that reinforced it. For example, a visual mnemonic for doubles involves using picture flash cards of objects to learn the two times math facts. The flash cards may include pictures of a skateboard with two sets of two wheels, a six-pack of soda with two sets of three cans, and a toy spider with two sets of four legs. First, the students had to find the two in the math fact and then remember the double picture related to the number that provided the answer. In station three, the teachers used a variation of a rehearsal drill model/peer-tutoring format (Beirne-Smith, 1991; Burns, 2005). Here students worked in pairs and used flash cards to review multiplication facts (both known [90%] and unknown [10%]). One student acted as a tutor and presented a fact with the answer, which was then repeated by the other student. Then, the tutor

presented all problems without the answers to the second student—first in order and then randomly. The teachers worked with students in stations two and three, while the students worked independently in station one. In the teacher-led stations, the teachers charted the facts that students had mastered and/or were still learning to ensure students progressed over time. Ms. Thomas and Ms. Merced planned to use this format for the remainder of the year to practice and review other mathematics concepts.

One Teach, One Drift

The one teach, one drift co-teaching format is similar to one teach, one observe. However, in this structure, while one teacher is teaching, the other teacher is drifting throughout the classroom. Co-teachers use this structure as a way to check for student understanding. It allows the opportunity to provide one-to-one instruction to students who may be struggling with a particular concept (Friend, 2005).

Throughout the school year, Ms. Merced and Ms. Thomas asked students to write in a journal about various aspects of mathematics (Baxter et al., 2005). They used prompts to elicit students' feelings or opinions (e.g., How do you feel about . . .) and their mathematical thinking (e.g., Explain to a third grader how to solve a two-digit by two-digit multiplication problem. What strategies did you use to solve the word problem?). The teachers encouraged students to use words, pictures, and symbols to explain and describe their mathematical thinking. They also asked students to write in journals before, during, and after lessons. Occasionally, when students appeared confused during the middle of class, the teachers instructed them to write about their thoughts on a particular topic. After each prompt, Ms. Merced and Ms. Thomas examined the journals. Several times, students' journal writing enabled the teachers to identify those who misunderstood a mathematical concept. The teachers then addressed the students' misconceptions using the one teach, one drift structure.

During a guided practice portion of the lesson taught by Ms. Merced, Ms. Thomas (who was drifting) approached students identified as having misconceptions and difficulty learning the new content. Where necessary, she provided additional one-to-one assistance, such as reminding students about the first step to solve a problem, prompting students' use of a diagram to help understand the problem, or providing the definition of a concept to address students' difficulties and to ensure their understanding of the new material.

POTENTIAL CHALLENGES TO BLENDING CO-TEACHING AND RESEARCH-BASED PRACTICES

Teachers' knowledge of research-based instructional practices for mathematics is critical to create supportive classroom learning environments for students with and without disabilities (Hudson & Miller, 2006; Miller, 2002). The research-base limitations regarding mathematics instruction for students with disabilities creates potential challenges to successfully blending co-teaching and research-based practices. In particular, we acknowledge three concerns.

First, it may be difficult to identify research-based practices designed specifically for students with disabilities in some mathematical content areas and for all age groups. For example, there are very limited research-based practices for students with disabilities in the mathematical fields of geometry, algebra, and data and probability. Moreover, the majority of available research-based practices are designed for elementary or middle school students.

Second, some instructional practices, including those presented in this article, are not necessarily appropriate for all students or age groups. For example, Montague's *Solve It!* strategy was developed for middle school students and may not be appropriate for children in the primary grades (K–2). In addition, *Solve It!* is one of a number of problem-solving strategies (e.g., Schema-Based Instruction) available that teachers may choose for implementation in their classrooms. Using all practices may be too numerous and overwhelming and potentially could create confusion for some students. Thus, it may not be advisable to introduce students to more than one word problem-solving strategy for a given year.

Finally, existing research-based practices present a limited range of instructional strategies, such as drill and practice and strategy instruction for solving word problems. It is also possible that some practices may not lend themselves to co-teaching structures or general education settings. With this in mind, we offer suggestions (see Figure 1) to address these concerns. Also, Figure 2 provides resources for supplementary research-based instructional practices to teach mathematics to students with disabilities.

PROMOTING CO-TEACHING PRACTICES AMONG GENERAL AND SPECIAL EDUCATION TEACHERS

Co-teaching requires thoughtful planning and consideration to ensure students' success in heterogeneous classrooms and to provide appropriate support for teachers (Walther-Thomas, 1997). Planning is integral to successful co-teaching and implementation of the instructional practices described in this article. However, the biggest challenge to co-teaching is allocating time for teachers to plan (Walther-Thomas; Sileo, 2003). As one teacher stated, "We have co-planning time together—without this time, co-teaching would be very difficult" (Magiera, Smith, Zigmond, & Gebauer, 2005, p. 22). Teachers are busy teaching throughout the day and after school meeting with parents and colleagues about school-related issues. As a result, it is difficult to plan together and planning often occurs "on the fly." According to Magiera et al., co-teachers are not successful when they do not have proper time to meet and discuss curriculum and instructional practices. Therefore, Murawski and Dieker (2004) suggest (a) planning together at least twice a

Figure 1. Suggestions for Blending Co-Teaching and Research-Based Practices

- Teachers may modify instructional practices to complement students' specific ages and instructional needs. For example, they may use a middle school/secondary level problem-solving strategy with elementary children by reducing the number of steps and simplifying the vocabulary. (We offer caution with modifying any research-based strategy as this may reduce its effectiveness. It is preferable to use age-appropriate practices, where possible.)

- Teachers may adapt special education research-based practices from other content areas when teaching mathematics. For instance, they may use a reading vocabulary technique, such as reciprocal teaching to help promote students' understanding and retention of key mathematical concepts (van Garderen, 2004).

- Teachers may use general mathematics education research-based practices to supplement or address topics not covered specifically for students with disabilities. If necessary, they can restructure the strategy by providing additional opportunities for guided practice that address specific needs of students with disabilities.

- Teachers may incorporate instructional strategies, within different co-teaching structures, that have been documented to work with children with disabilities (Cobb Morocco, 2001; Fuchs & Fuchs, 2001; Maccini & Gagnon, 2000; Montague, 1998). These practices include but are not limited to (a) teacher modeling, such as thinking aloud while problem solving; (b) providing opportunities for practice and cumulative review that involves new and previously learned materials; (c) offering immediate and corrective feedback, as well as continuous monitoring of student performance; (d) using authentic tasks to promote students' ability to generalize learning; (e) teaching students how to use cognitive and meta-cognitive strategies, such as different representational forms (e.g., symbols, concrete objects, and diagrams) to reinforce mathematical concepts and solve word problems; and (f) promoting use of dialogue and communication as well as social mediation strategies, such as peer-tutoring and cooperative learning.

week; (b) discussing content and how it will be taught; (c) using a common plan book; and (d) including lessons where special educators take the lead in planning and instruction.

Another challenge associated with co-teaching relates to scheduling opportunities, particularly if the special education teacher must work in general education settings and within a resource-based classroom. One possible solution involves clustering students and allowing them to travel from class to class for instruction, thereby decreasing the number of classrooms rather than the number of students who receive services (Walther-Thomas, 1997). For example, rather than requiring students to attend the resource room for instruction, Ms. Merced provided services to some students in Ms. Thomas's

Figure 2. Supplementary Information About Research-Based Practices and Other Ideas for Teaching Mathematics

Allsopp, D. H., Kyger, M. M., & Lovin, L. H. (2007). *Teaching mathematics meaningfully: Solutions for reaching struggling learners.* Baltimore, MD: Paul. H. Brookes.

Gurganus, S. P. (2007). *Math instruction for students with learning problems.* Boston, MA: Allyn & Bacon.

Hudson, P., & Miller, S. P. (2006). *Designing and implementing mathematics instruction for students with diverse learning needs.* Boston, MA: Allyn & Bacon.

Jitendra, A. (2002). Teaching students math problem solving through graphic representations. *TEACHING Exceptional Children, 34*(4), 34-38.

Miller, S. P., & Hudson, P. J. (2006). Helping students with disabilities understand what mathematics means. *TEACHING Exceptional Children, 39*(1), 28–35.

Montague, M., & Jitendra, A. K. (2006). *Teaching mathematics to middle school students with learning difficulties.* New York, NY: The Guilford Press.

Montague, M., Warger, C., & Morgan, H. (2000) Solve it! Strategy instruction to improve mathematical problem solving. *Learning Disabilities Research and Practice, 15,* 110–116.

classroom. This approach allowed Ms. Merced the opportunity to increase the level and intensity of services she afforded students in a general education setting.

The co-teaching structures presented in this article may not work for all teachers. Further, it may be advisable for teachers to implement one structure at a time. Teachers can implement different structures as they develop collegial relationships and a comfort level working together. Throughout the year, Ms. Merced and Ms. Thomas became more comfortable co-teaching and eventually implemented lessons that utilized all co-teaching structures. Essentially, no one co-teaching structure is better than another. It is also possible to use the structures for different instructional purposes and to (a) pre-teach concepts, (b) re-teach information taught previously, (c) review content, (d) make up material missed during students' absences, (e) provide enrichment activities, (f) allow students to pursue specific interests, and (g) assess students' progress in developing skills and understanding critical concepts (Cook & Friend, 1995). See Figure 3 for additional information about co-teaching and suggestions for implementation.

Finally, another challenge that may arise between general and special education teachers and hinder co-teaching efforts, particularly in mathematics, relates to different philosophies of instruction (Parmar & DeSimone, 2006) that influence their instructional recommendations for students with and without disabilities. A tension that often exists concerns teachers'

Figure 3. Additional Print and Nonprint Resources About Co-Teaching

---

Print Resources

Dieker, L. A. (2006). The coteaching lesson plan book (3rd ed.). *Knowledge by Design:* Whitefish Bay, WI.

Friend, M. (2005). *Power of Two* [DVD/Video]. Bloomington: Indiana University. A Forum on Education.

Friend, M., & Cook, L. (2006). *Interactions: Collaboration skills for school professionals* (5th ed.). Boston, MA: Allyn & Bacon.

Murawski, W. W. (2005). *Co-teaching for success: Effective strategies for working together in today's inclusive classrooms.* Bellevue, WA: Bureau of Education and Research.

Villa, R. A., Thousand, J. S., & Nevin, A. I. (2008). *A Guide to co-teaching: Practical tips for facilitating student learning* (2nd ed.). Thousand Oaks, CA: Corwin Press.

Internet Resources

http://www.2teachllc.com/index.html
This Web site provides lesson plans and information about professional development opportunities for teachers who work in co-teaching classrooms (K–12).

http://www.marilynfriend.com/
This Web site provides resources for teachers and administrators who want more information on co-teaching.

---

specific ideas regarding the one best approach for teaching students with disabilities. For example, many special education teachers and researchers may support explicit teaching methodologies in contrast to inquiry-based or reform-based approaches (Hudson, Miller, & Butler, 2006). No one tactic is the best for students with disabilities, and it may be appropriate to blend practices to attain students' goals and objectives (Karp & Voltz, 2000). Parmar and DeSimone recommend that teachers discuss their individual perspectives as a way to understand various points of view. Possible discussion topics include, but are not limited to, inquiry versus direct/explicit instruction; using particular motivators, grading systems, and grouping practices; and scheduling and pacing curricular content (Parmar & DeSimone).

SUMMARY

Co-teaching structures can benefit students and teachers. Nevertheless, although structures can enhance student learning, it is also important to consider the subject matter. General and special educators can work together to blend their knowledge bases. This relationship is invaluable because it weds content and strategy specialists, and allows teachers an opportunity to meet all students' mathematical learning needs.

REFERENCES

Argüelles, M. E., Hughes, M. T., & Schumm, J. S. (2000). Co-teaching: A different approach to inclusion. *Principal, 79*(4), 48, 50–51.

Baxter, J. A., Woodward, J., & Olson, D. (2005). Writing in mathematics: An alternative form of communication for academically low-achieving students. *Learning Disabilities Research and Practice, 20,* 119–135.

Beirne-Smith, M. (1991). Peer tutoring in arithmetic for children with learning disabilities. *Exceptional Children, 57,* 330–339.

Burns, M. K. (2005). Using incremental rehearsal to increase fluency of single-digit multiplication facts with children identified as learning disabled in mathematics computation. *Education and Treatment of Children, 28,* 237–249.

Cass, M., Cates, D., Smith, M., & Jackson, C. (2003). Effects of manipulative instruction on solving area and perimeter problems by students with learning disabilities. *Learning Disabilities Research and Practice, 18,* 112–120.

Cobb Morocco, C. (2001). Teaching for understanding with students with disabilities: New directions for research on access to the general education curriculum. *Learning Disability Quarterly, 24,* 5–13.

Cook, L., & Friend, M. (1995). Co-teaching: Guidelines for creating effective practices. *Focus on Exceptional Children, 28*(3), 1–16.

Fontana, K. C. (2005). The effects of co-teaching on the achievement of eighth grade students with learning disabilities. *The Journal of At Risk Issues, 11*(2), 17–23.

Friend, M. (2005). *Power of two* [DVD/Video]. Bloomington: Indiana University. A Forum on Education.

Friend, M., & Cook, L. (2006). *Interactions: Collaboration skills for school professionals* (5th ed.). Boston, MA: Allyn & Bacon.

Friend, M., & Reising, M. (1993). Co-teaching: An overview of the past, a glimpse at the present, and considerations for the future. *Preventing School Failure, 37*(4), 6–11.

Fuchs, L. S., & Fuchs, D. (2001). Principles for the prevention and intervention of mathematics difficulties. *Learning Disabilities Research and Practice, 16,* 85–95.

Gately, S. E., & Gately, F. J. (2001). Understanding coteaching components. *TEACHING Exceptional Children, 33*(4), 40–47.

Geary, D. C. (2004). Mathematics and learning disabilities. *Journal of Learning Disabilities, 37,* 4–15.

Hudson, P., & Miller, S. P. (2006). *Designing and implementing mathematics instruction for students with diverse learning needs.* Boston, MA: Allyn & Bacon.

Hudson, P., Miller, S. P., & Butler, F. (2006). Adapting and merging instruction within reform based mathematics classrooms. *American Secondary Education, 35*(1), 19–32.

Individuals With Disabilities Education Improvement Act of 2004. Pub. L. 108–446.

Jang, S. J. (2006). Research on the effects of team teaching upon two secondary school teachers. *Educational Research, 48*(2), 177–194.

Jitendra, A. (2002). Teaching students math problem-solving through graphic representations. *TEACHING Exceptional Children, 34*(4), 34–38.

Karp, K. S., & Voltz, D. L. (2000). Weaving mathematical instructional strategies into inclusive settings. *Intervention in School and Clinic, 35*(4), 206–215.

Kohler-Evans, P. (2006). Co-teaching: How to make this marriage work in front of the kids. *Education, 127*(2), 260–264.

Kroesbergen, E. H., & van Luit, J. E. H. (2003). Mathematics interventions for children with special needs: A meta-analysis. *Remedial and Special Education, 24,* 97–114.

Maccini, P., & Gagnon, J. C. (2000). Best practices for teaching mathematics to secondary students with special needs. *Focus on Exceptional Children, 32*, 1–22.

Magiera, K., Smith, C., Zigmond, N., & Gebauer, K. (2005). Benefits of co-teaching in secondary mathematics classes. *TEACHING Exceptional Children, 37*(3), 20–24.

McLaughlin, T. F., & Skinner, C. H. (1996). Improving academic performance through self-management: Cover, copy, and compare. *Intervention in School and Clinic, 32*(2), 113–118.

Miller, S. P. (2002). *Validated practices for teaching students with diverse needs and abilities.* Boston, MA: Allyn & Bacon.

Miller, S. P., Harris, C., Strawser, S., Jones, W. P., & Mercer, C. (1998). Teaching multiplication to second graders in inclusive settings. *Focus of Learning Problems in Mathematics, 20*, 50–70.

Miller, S. P., Mercer, C. D., & Dillon, A. (1992). Acquiring and retaining math skills. *Intervention, 28*, 105–110.

Montague, M. (1998). Mathematics instruction in diverse classrooms. In K. R. Harris, S. Graham, and D. Deshler (Eds.). *Teaching every child every day: Learning in diverse schools and classrooms* (pp. 168–207). Cambridge, MA: Brookline Books.

Montague, M., & van Garderen, D. (2008). Evidence-based interventions for students with learning and behavioral challenges. In R. J. Morris and N. Mather (Eds.). *Research-based practice for effective mathematics instruction* (pp. 236–257). New York, NY: Taylor & Francis.

Montague, M., Warger, C., & Morgan, H. (2000). Solve it! Strategy instruction to improve mathematical problem solving. *Learning Disabilities Research and Practice, 15*, 110–116.

Murawski, W. W., & Dieker, L. A. (2004). Tips and strategies for co-teaching at the secondary level. *TEACHING Exceptional Children, 36*(5), 52–58.

No Child Left Behind Act. Pub. L. 107–110, 115 Stat. 1425 (2001).

Pape, S. J., & Tchoshanov, M. A. (2001). The role of representation(s) in developing mathematical understanding. *Theory into Practice, 40*, 118–127. doi: 10.1207/s15 430421tip4002_6

Parmar, R. S. & DeSimone, J. R. (2006). Facilitating teacher collaboration in middle school mathematics classrooms with special-needs students. In M. Montague and A. Jitendra (Eds.), *Middle school students with mathematics difficulties* (pp. 154–174). New York, NY: Guilford Press.

Pearl, C. E., & Miller, K. J. (2007). Co-taught middle school mathematics classrooms: Accommodations and enhancements for students with specific learning disabilities. *Focus on Learning Problems in Mathematics, 29*(2), 1–20.

Ripley, S., (1997). *Collaboration between general and special education teachers.* (ERIC Digest). (ERIC Document Reproduction Service No. ED409317). Retrieved from www.eric.ed.gov

Salend, S. J. (2008). *Creating inclusive classrooms: Effective and reflective practices for all students* (6th ed.). Upper Saddle River, NJ: Pearson.

Silberman, M. (1996). *Active learning: 101 strategies to teach any subject.* Needham Heights, MA: Allyn & Bacon.

Sileo, J. M. (2003). Co-teaching: Rationale for best practices. *Journal of Asia–Pacific Special Education, 3*(1), 17–26.

Skinner, C. H., Ford, J. M., & Yunker, B. D. (1991). A comparison of instructional response requirements on the multiplication performance of behaviorally disordered students. *Behavioral Disorders, 17*, 56–65.

U.S. Department of Education. (2006). *Twenty-fourth annual report to Congress on the implementation of IDEA.* Washington, DC: Author.

van Garderen, D. (2004). Reciprocal teaching as a comprehension strategy for understanding mathematical word problems. *Reading and Writing Quarterly: Overcoming Learning Difficulties, 20*(2), 225–229.

van Garderen, D., Scheuermann, A., Jackson, C., & Hampton, D. (2009). Supporting collaboration between general educators and special educators to teach students who struggle with mathematics: A review of recent empirical literature. *Psychology in the Schools, 46*(1), 56–77.

Villa, R. A., Thousand, J. S., & Nevin, A. I. (2008). *A guide to co-teaching: Practical tips for facilitating student learning* (2nd ed.). Thousand Oaks, CA: Corwin Press.

Walther-Thomas, C. (1997). Co-teaching experiences: The benefits and problems that teachers and principals report over time. *Journal of Learning Disabilities, 30*(4), 395–407.

Watson, A. (2002). Instances of mathematical thinking among low attaining students in an ordinary secondary classroom. *Journal of Mathematical Behavior, 20,* 461–475.

Witzel, B., Smith, S. W., & Brownell, M. T. (2001). How can I help students with learning disabilities in algebra? *Intervention in School and Clinic, 31,* 101–104.

Wood, D. K., Frank, A. R., & Wacker, D. P. (1998). Teaching multiplication facts to students with learning disabilities. *Journal of Applied Behavior Analysis, 31,* 323–338.

Xin, Y. P., & Jitendra, A. K. (2006). Teaching problem-solving skills to middle school students with learning difficulties: Schema-based strategy instruction. In M. Montague & A. Jitendra (Eds.), *Teaching mathematics to middle school students with learning difficulties* (pp. 51–71). New York, NY: Guilford Press.

Originally published in *TEACHING Exceptional Children*, Vol. 42, No. 3, 14–21.

6

Co-Instructing at the Secondary Level: Strategies for Success

Nancy Rice, Elizabeth Drame, Laura Owens, Elise M. Frattura

As students with disabilities increasingly spend instructional time in general education classrooms, more and more special educators are working there as well. Through interviews and classroom observations, we found that effective special education co-teachers share certain characteristics: professionalism, the ability to articulate and model instruction to meet student needs, the ability to accurately assess student progress, the ability to analyze teaching/teaching styles, the ability to work with a wide range of students, and a vested interest in course content.

Much has been written about collaboration and co-teaching in secondary settings, including the importance of understanding your partner's teaching approach (Keefe, Moore, & Duff, 2004; Murawski, 2003); determining readiness to co-teach (Bradley, King-Sears & Tessier-Switlick, 1997; Murawski); clarifying roles, responsibilities, and expectations (Friend & Bursuck, 2002; Murawski & Dieker, 2004; Murray, 2004); scheduling shared planning time (Friend & Cook, 2002); and effective communication, including constructive dialogue and conflict resolution (Wood, 1998).

The Individuals With Disabilities Education Improvement Act of 2004 (IDEA 2004) underscores what the No Child Left Behind Act (NCLB) and IDEA 1997 mandated: Instruction in special education must be tied as closely as possible to the general education curriculum. Under NCLB, students with disabilities are now required to take content area exams; student success is increasingly dependent upon effective co-teaching in general education class-rooms.

IDEA 2004's definition of "highly qualified special education teacher" in the secondary school setting incorporates both special education certification and demonstration of content knowledge. In addition, the definition specifically addresses special education teachers who provide "consultative services" to content-area teachers. In these instances, the technical expertise of the special educator (rather than core content knowledge) is deemed critical (National Education Association, n.d.). The assumption in both cases is that special educators will go into a general education classroom, size up the situation in terms of student needs and content delivery, and make relevant, concrete suggestions that will aid student understanding, retention, and/or application of concepts. Are there particular skills and attributes that aid special educators in co-teaching or consultative situations?

WHAT DO TEACHERS SAY ABOUT CO-TEACHING?

As part of a larger study, we investigated how a K–12 district was able to sustain a policy of inclusive education for a 12-year period. We conducted focus group and individual interviews with general and special educators (all of whom had been involved in co-teaching situations), as well as classroom observations of these teachers in action (see box, "About the Study"). Both special and general educators stressed the importance of co-teaching for sustaining inclusive practices; they also provided examples of what was helpful to them in a co-teaching situation.

In addition, all of the authors are former special educators in secondary settings, one of us is a former mentor to special educators, and two of us have worked in special education administration. All of us currently work in preparing professionals—teachers or administrators—to work in schools. Our experiences include urban, suburban, and rural schools. From the literature and our own experience, we know that support for teaming varies widely among school districts and buildings, from clear administrative support for co-teaching to separate case loads and a lack of physical proximity. However, we have seen co-teachers succeed in a variety of contexts. Naturally, teaming is easier when supports such as shared planning time are intentionally scheduled, but even in those instances, not every teacher is necessarily on board with the concept of working closely with another educator. Conversely, even in environments designed to separate special and general education students and educators, teachers do find ways to collaborate for the purpose of serving students better.

In our research, general educators noted that their most effective co-teaching relationships were with special education teachers who had strengths in six specific areas: professionalism; ability to articulate and model instruction to meet student needs; ability to accurately assess student progress; ability to analyze teaching/teaching styles; ability to work with a

About the Study

The interviews and observations described in this article were conducted as part of a larger study of a suburban district in the Midwest with 4,500 students. Participants (13 special educators, 18 general educators, 5 teaching assistants, 4 counselor/school psychologists, 3 teacher-leaders, and 3 administrators) were representative in terms of subject area, grade level, and number of years of experience in education. Teachers were also representative in terms of the types of students they worked with, ranging from students with learning disabilities to those with significant cognitive disabilities.

The authors conducted ten 30- to 45-minute focus groups of 4 to 6 participants each; six individual interviews; and 40 hours of observation in classroom and other school settings.

We categorized our transcripts of audiotaped interviews by topics frequently mentioned by participants. The data presented in this article were coded under "co-teaching" and sub-categorized as "strategies" and "important practices."

wide range of students; and knowledge of, or interest in developing knowledge of, course content (see Figure 1).

1. PROFESSIONALISM

General educators said that the ability to plan was essential for success. When working with a co-teacher, they appreciated being able to count on their colleague to attend classes daily and to let them know in advance of any absences. Particularly once a routine has been established, classroom teachers and students count on the presence of both teachers.

Case Study: Tom and Ben

Tom, a special educator, was less than confident in his role as a co-teacher in a science classroom; his co-teacher, Ben, was less than welcoming. Tom began using the period to catch up on paperwork. Initially, he let Ben know when an "emergency" came up, but as the semester wore on, Tom began to think of the science period as his time to consult with teachers, test students, and draft IEPs. In December, Ben brought the issue to a faculty meeting, much to Tom's chagrin. Tom realized at that point that his "skipping out" on his responsibility to a colleague and his students had not only marred his reputation, but also had hampered the progress of co-teaching in the building as a whole.

It took time to repair the damage done by this situation, which fueled the fires of some who felt they were the "real" teachers and that special educators were superfluous. At the same time, it highlighted the importance of general educators' professionalism in actively working with a colleague to develop a role for him or her in the classroom. Consistency and professional

Figure 1. Essential Aspects of Effective Co-Teaching

1. Professionalism: build credibility	Be consistent. Show up on time and every day.
	Be courteous. Let partner teachers know if you're not going to be there.
	Be informative. Suggest and model alternate methods of instruction, lessons, themes, connections to other content areas. Provide information on individual student needs, curricular modifications, and new software programs.
	Be proactive. Anticipate what you can do to enhance lessons and the instructional environment.
2. Articulate and model instruction to meet student needs	Be specific. Explain how particular instructional strategies impact students with certain difficulties and suggest alternatives.
	Be analytical. Conduct a skill task analysis or a functional behavior analysis. Teach students the prerequisite skills necessary to acquire a higher-order skill or to effect a change in behavior.
	Be exemplary. Model reinforcement of positive behavior change.
3. Accurately assess student progress	Be helpful. Volunteer to help with grading to enhance understanding of course expectations and range of student performance. Work with student to teach the grading system and to help him/her succeed in understanding course content.
	Be resourceful. Connect student IEP goals to course expectations. Develop at least two methods of assessment, combining IEP goals and course content. With general educator, select the most appropriate method of assessment. Present to IEP team.
4. Analyze teaching/ teaching styles	Be observant. Point out classroom nuances to assist students in organizing information and seeing patterns in a teacher's practices.
	Show your co-teacher how she can make routines and expectations more explicit for students, and explain how and why this can be helpful.
5. Work with a wide range of students	Be creative. Use knowledge of learning styles to adapt traditional lesson formats.
	Be innovative. Use opportunities, such as assistive technology, to aid in bridging the learning styles between and among students. Educate both instructors and students about different learning styles.
6. Knowledge of course content	Be honest about your background. Many special educators don't have a degree in math or English—no one expects you to!
	Be curious. Ask what you could be reading; borrow a teacher's edition of the textbook; use Internet, library, and other resources to develop your background knowledge of a subject.
	Be prepared. Have a clear concept of the main ideas/the main goals of the lesson/unit. Focus on these with a small group so students can participate in whole-class discussions.
	Be a co-learner. Use your own process of learning to identify where students might get stuck; share materials that you used in your "review" with students and teachers; make connections to other content areas; show how core ideas apply to "real life" or current events.

courtesy are essential for any professional relationship. Although this may seem to be obvious, the importance of courtesy and professionalism cannot be emphasized enough; they go a long way toward laying a foundation for a strong co-teaching relationship. With this strong foundation, additional information that you share with your colleagues is more likely to be received positively.

Another aspect of professionalism noted by general education teachers was special educators' ability to be proactive in introducing new ideas regarding curriculum, instruction, interdisciplinary connections, assistive technology, and strategies to address the needs of individual learners.

2. ABILITY TO ARTICULATE AND MODEL INSTRUCTION TO MEET STUDENT NEEDS

Co-teaching provides opportunities for teachers to bring together their areas of expertise to benefit all students in a general education classroom. It is not enough to tell a general education teacher that a student has a learning disability. The important information is: what does the label mean in terms of teaching and reaching that student?

Case Study: Julia and Steve

Devon had language processing difficulties. Getting the key points from a lecture delivered auditorily was difficult for him, as was reading a chapter and answering questions. For Marketha, a student with visual-motor processing difficulties, note taking and written responses were difficult, as she focused on and was anxious about writing—missing the content. Julia, a special educator, worked with Steve, Devon and Marketha's English teacher. The lesson focused on character analysis, specifically Lenny in John Steinbeck's *Of Mice and Men*. Steve had planned a lesson wherein students would write a paragraph for each of three selected passages, discussing what each passage indicated about Lenny's character. Students would hand in three paragraphs at the end of class.

Julia suggested that the lesson be modified for the entire class, incorporating a cooperative grouping arrangement, "think-pair-share." After reading the first passage, students wrote up to three words describing Lenny and explained to a partner why they chose those words. Julia and Steve circulated during the paired discussions to assess and aid student understanding of the material. After another passage was read, students were asked to write two words or phrases: one that defined Lenny and another that indicated how they came to that characterization. After a third reading, the students' homework assignment was to write a paragraph explaining how the final reading had characterized Lenny. For this assignment, students had the option of following a paragraph structure Julia modeled (e.g., "On p. 167, Lenny said, "_____." This shows that he was _____ because _____.").

Julia was able to show Steve how Devon and Marketha could participate in the key content of the lesson, once it was adapted for language and visual-motor processing difficulties. Activities were short and clear, and focused on key concepts: one or two aspects of the character. The goal of the lesson remained the same, but students could focus on salient aspects of the text, rather than struggle with sifting through inessential details or with a difficult writing task.

Case Study: Sara and Chad

Sara teamed with Chad, a history teacher. Chad was personable, funny, and technology-savvy. He typically used PowerPoint slides along with his engaging lectures, which were filled with stories and little-known facts. Toward the end of October, Chad wanted his students to learn note taking in preparation for college. He continued using PowerPoint, but for several days included only main headings. Following that, students took notes on their own. Chad found that many had fared poorly; some had not written down the most important ideas.

Sara volunteered to teach "selecting relevant from irrelevant information" and note taking for the next 2 weeks. She took notes during Chad's lecture and shared these with the class during the final 15 minutes of the period. Sara, Chad, and the students discussed which aspects of the lecture were important enough to note, and why; and which could be ignored, and why. She also provided tips such as drawing pictures to remember concepts such as "The Constitutional Convention" and using "CC," "w/," initials (BF for Benjamin Franklin) and other abbreviations.

Case Study: Liz and Ryan

Liz's work in Ryan's classroom provides another example of modeling instruction. Tracy, a ninth-grade student with social skill, self-regulation, and self-control deficits, was verbally disruptive in her general education math class on a regular basis. Liz, Tracy's special education teacher, conducted a functional behavioral analysis to identify the antecedents of Tracy's emotional outbursts. Using this data, the IEP team determined that Tracy became frustrated when she experienced difficulty following instructions or performing individual academic tasks.

The team developed a behavior intervention plan including several strategies to be reinforced by Ryan, the math teacher, that would increase Tracy's ability to monitor her own emotions and behaviors. Liz modeled the reinforcement of a strategy that required Tracy to recognize when she was beginning to get frustrated and to ask for a pass to spend 10 minutes discussing her frustration with the school psychologist or Liz herself. She also modeled reinforcement of Tracy's self-monitoring, which required Tracy to assess how she was doing at 15-minute intervals.

Because Ryan was skeptical about his own ability to consistently implement these strategies (although he saw tremendous growth in Tracy's ability to control her outbursts when Liz was assisting with the reinforcement), Liz and Ryan took turns implementing the two strategies over a 2-week period. Ryan's success at reinforcing these strategies was directly related to Tracy taking increasing responsibility for her behavior. In addition, this situation increased Ryan's confidence and skill in being able to implement unfamiliar strategies.

3. ABILITY TO ACCURATELY ASSESS STUDENT PROGRESS

In our interviews, general educators admitted to needing guidance regarding fair assessment and grading of students with IEPs. The special educator can provide valuable direction in how to fairly assess and grade these students— but this requires a thorough knowledge of both the individual students and the grading system used by general educators in different content classes.

Volunteering to help with grading provides insight into key concepts and primary expectations of the course, as well as the range of performance of the entire class—necessary to develop ways of modifying progress assessment for IEP students and explaining the grading scheme to general education colleagues.

Case Study: Kathy

In one middle school, Kathy worked with the general educators to develop *mastery-level* or *criterion grading*, in which the content for the unit was divided into subcomponents. Students earned credit when their mastery of a certain skill or knowledge base reached an acceptable level.

Case Study: Marietta

Marietta worked with general educators on *level grading*. Using subscripts to indicate the level of difficulty on which the student's grade was based individualized the grading system. For example, if a student earned a B_5, this indicated that the student had earned a B on material at the fifth-grade level.

Case Study: Brian

In a ninth-grade government class, Brian worked with teachers using *shared grading*. The general education teacher determined 60% of a student's grade (calculated in the same way other students were graded) and Brian determined 40% of the grade, which was based on the student's IEP goals.

Case Study: Colette

Colette used a *portfolio approach* and *rubrics* in an English class. For essay writing, she adapted a writing rubric that she found on the Web and gave it to all students. The rubric laid out several areas to be assessed (clarity of ideas, supporting evidence, transitions, grammar, etc.). For each assessment category, columns on the rubric described varying levels of performance—ranging from *not evident* to *advanced*—and what these looked like, as well as their correlation to a letter grade (A–F). Students had nine writing assignments throughout the semester that were assessed using the rubric. The first six of these were used to provide feedback on performance and to articulate to students how to move to the next level. The final three rubrics were averaged together for their final course grade. This system was consistent with IEP goals for improving written language.

4. ABILITY TO ANALYZE TEACHING/TEACHING STYLES

Barbara, an English teacher, told us, "The [special education co-teachers] observe idiosyncrasies about the way I teach, and how I do business, and that's useful to kids who come to my classes as well." Barbara's observation is subtle but important in identifying ways to help students succeed in general education settings. How general educators convey information, how they structure their classrooms, and what their expectations are is valuable information for students. Although students may experience a routine opening activity every day or see a test date listed on the board, they may not realize how to use this information.

Co-teachers are in the unique position of pointing out taken-for-granted classroom structures, teacher practices, and curriculum materials that can be useful in helping students plan and organize information and master skills and strategies. Pointing out to students what to pay attention to and teaching them how to "read" clues as to what is important in a given classroom can aid student success in general education classrooms. Special educators can also share this information with general educators, who can then make their practices and expectations explicit for all students.

Case Study: Kyle

Kyle co-taught in two classes, math and English. The math teacher was very focused on tests and not too concerned if students turned in homework on time, whereas the English teacher was a stickler for turning in homework and did not put much weight on exams. Kyle explained to the students that if they had homework in both classes on a particular night, their English homework should take priority. When it came to studying for tests, they should focus their efforts on math. Furthermore, both teachers listed homework and test dates on the board. Kyle instructed students to write these in their weekly planners and to block out time on the two evenings prior to due dates in order to schedule time to complete the tasks.

Case Study: Jeff and Deb

Jeff, a special educator, co-taught with Deb, an English teacher. Deb began each class with a warm-up activity of grammar and punctuation corrections. Students needed to identify and correct sentences with errors. Deb reviewed these with the class after the majority of students had finished working individually. Jeff had worked with Deb in previous semesters, so he knew that some of these same (or very similar) items would appear on the bi-weekly quizzes. He helped his students with IEPs to designate a section in their English folder for these daily sheets and to use them as study guides for quizzes.

Case Study: Carolyn and Frank

Carolyn worked with Frank, a science teacher. Frank was a very systematic teacher. He followed a similar structure for each chapter: introduce vocabulary, teach main concepts, conduct a lab experiment, answer questions, review, and test. He used the publisher's tests, which all had a similar format (e.g., vocabulary assessed via matching; main concepts assessed by short answer); Frank typically added an essay question regarding the lab. Carolyn supported her students by anticipating lessons ahead of time and letting them practice the format of the test; once comfortable with the format, the students could focus on the content.

5. ABILITY TO WORK WITH A WIDE RANGE OF STUDENTS

Morgan, a general educator, said, "The best people that I've had come into my classroom have really taken a role, not just to be with their two, or three, or four students. They pick up on what your class is like, and then, they're there for everybody, and I think it makes the special education students more comfortable too, because the special education teacher isn't just there and focused on them the whole time. So it makes it easier for the entire class; . . . they're there as a co-teacher, which is huge."

It is critical that the special education teacher be seen as another teacher and not just a "helper" for students with disabilities. In some settings, part of the co-teacher's role may be to educate both instructors and students as to different learning styles.

Case Study: Liz

Liz, a special educator, and John, a general educator, collaborated to integrate assistive technology in a ninth-grade language arts classroom. Reviewing the quality of the writing produced by both special and general education students, the two teachers concluded that much improvement was needed. The school had access to assistive technology software such as Draft Builder and Inspiration. Liz had training on the use of these software programs and strategies for integrating the software into instruction; she worked with John to develop lessons that included exposure to the software for all students, using the classroom computers.

One of the students in the class, Rosanna, had trouble producing quality assignments due to written language difficulties. Liz worked closely with Rosanna on the writing process, with particular emphasis on brainstorming and organizing ideas. When the time came to put pen to paper, Rosanna's fine-motor difficulties prevented her from generating more than one to two sentences, despite the depth of content generated during brainstorming. However, when Liz took Rosanna to the computer lab for 1 hour a day for 1 week, Rosanna was able to write three fully developed paragraphs with very little assistance. Liz used this written product to convince John that an Alphasmart, a portable word processor, was a necessity for her and not a "crutch," and successfully advocated for including the use of an Alphasmart in Rosanna's IEP.

The general education students were taught the integrated technology lessons at the same time Rosanna began using the Alphasmart. The general education students were very excited about their ability to use technology throughout the writing process. The increased use of technology in the classroom both captured student attention and resulted in much more depth and productivity in all the students' written products.

Case Study: Renee

Renee, a special educator, co-taught in a history class. Her co-teacher believed that all students should follow his lectures by taking notes; he did not believe in providing students with "crutches" such as handouts with part of the lecture outlined. Renee negotiated with her co-teacher to teach a lesson on note taking. She began by introducing the notion of multiple intelligences. Via a self-test, students determined their areas of strength. Renee then explained how the students could use their strengths during a lecture. For those with strong linguistic or auditory intelligences, the process of synthesizing information and writing down key ideas—taking notes—helps retain information (in addition to having notes for later review). For those with a strong visual intelligence, notes with drawings or graphic organizers are helpful. For those with attention difficulties (perhaps a strong kinesthetic intelligence which makes listening to long lectures difficult), a handout with a skeletal outline would be useful to help them stay on track during the period. These students also may want to do some systematic stretching during the period, beginning with their feet, then their ankles, legs, arms, hands, and neck. Renee had all the students stretch in their seats, and explained that this could help individuals who have a strong need for movement without distracting others. Students might also ask the instructor if they can get up periodically to walk around the room.

Renee helped all of the students, and her colleague, understand that "sameness" was not "equal" (and not necessarily helpful) to all learners.

Some students may learn best by taking their own notes in traditional outline format; others may record the information from a lecture in their notebooks visually, or benefit from a template that provides an overall structure; still others may be helped by having an outline highlighting the main points. Through this lesson, Renee helped all the students better understand their individual learning styles, setting the stage for effective self-advocacy.

In both of these cases, Liz and Renee were able to work with the entire class. Liz helped John to see how student productivity could be improved using assistive technology, whereas Renee helped students to increase their own self-understanding regarding their dominant learning style. Renee hoped to help both students and her co-teacher to see that different learning styles are natural and inevitable; therefore, different teaching styles should also be the norm.

6. KNOWLEDGE OF COURSE CONTENT

Tamika, a high school math teacher explained,

> One thing that I really appreciated anytime that I've ever had any of the special education people in my classroom is that they're there to help the kids, so they really want to learn math, too. When they go back to the resource room, if they have other kids that are in geometry classes, and we're all kind of doing the same stuff, they're more confident in their ability to help, because they've been working on it along with the kids. They take notes, they have their own notebooks, they have their own book. I think they work hard to learn [the material] and they can help their students so much better if they can understand the material, so I appreciate that.

Co-teachers are often assigned to content area classrooms outside their own area(s) of expertise. However, the most successful co-teachers review the content outside of the classroom.

Case Study: Joan

To her surprise (and dismay!), Joan was scheduled to co-teach in a Grade 11 health class during second quarter. The curriculum was bodily systems and infectious and communicable diseases. She "studied up" on the systems of the body and on the diseases presented in the text. Because of her recently relearned knowledge of the course content, she could more easily modify lessons, homework, and expectations for her IEP students. For instance, instead of requiring some students to identify all parts of the body, she required identification of only those parts that were necessary for understanding bodily functions (covered later in the quarter).

Joan consulted with her co-teacher and introduced visual aids and Web sites she had used in her own recent studies, to illustrate bodily systems. In addition, she brought in news items twice a week, adding both a literacy dimension and real-world application for the understanding of diseases, how they can spread, and how they might be contained.

Case Study: Jarad and Brian

Brian was a special education teacher co-teaching an English class with Jarad, an energetic theatre teacher. Of the 40 students in the class, 11 had IEPs, and the majority of these students required assistance with written language. For a 3-week curriculum unit on comparative essays, the class would read four different speeches (one each by "Fighting Bob" LaFollette, Russ Feingold, Frederick Douglass, and Barack Obama), perform the speeches, conduct research in small groups on the context in which each politician spoke, and make connections between and among the speeches.

Jarad provided Brian with the speeches in December and told him he planned to use them in January. Neither an English nor a history major, Brian read the speeches, made notes, and did his own background research on the biographies of the speakers and the historical context of their impassioned speeches. This knowledge gave him confidence in working with all students in the classroom and provided him with the content he needed to be able to assist them in constructing their essays. Brian also co-taught in a history class and connected the speeches to the history content.

While Jarad made verbal connections during class performances, Brian supplemented these by highlighting the text on the overhead projector and making lists on the board. He listed the themes each politician focused on in their speeches. Over the course of several days, these lists grew longer and students were able to spot connections between speeches. After all the speeches had been performed, Brian spent 3 days modeling how to conceptualize, outline, and write a comparative essay of two speeches. The two co-teachers then worked with individual and small groups in developing and refining student essays.

FINAL THOUGHTS

Co-teaching provides students with opportunities to be consistently exposed to general education curricula and expectations while being supported to meet those expectations. Through relevant and challenging content, students can progress toward their IEP goals and gain content area knowledge that is often not available to them in special education classes.

Students, obviously, benefit from well-planned lessons; educators, too, have a tremendous amount of knowledge to gain through successful collaborative relationships. Special educators can increase their content area knowledge while general educators increase their ability to adapt lessons through

Additional Resources

Professionalism

Akerley, G. (n.d.). *10 tips for getting along with people at work.* Retrieved September 29, 2006, from http://www.fabjob.com/tips163.html

Keefe, E., B., & Moore, V. (2004). The challenge of co-teaching in inclusive classrooms at the high school level: What the teachers told us. *American Secondary Education, 32*(3), 77-88.

Articulate and Model Instructional Strategies

Edyburn, D. (2000). Assistive technology and students with mild disabilities. *Focus on Exceptional Children, 32*(9), 1–24.

Kim, A., Woodruff, A. L., Klein, C., Vaughn, S. (2006). Facilitating co-teaching for literacy in general education classrooms through technology: Focus on students with learning disabilities. *Reading & Writing Quarterly, 22,* 269–291.

Parette, P., & Wojcik, B. W. (2004). Creating a technology toolkit for students with mental retardation: A systematic approach. *Journal of Special Education Technology, 19*(4), 23–32.

Saskatoon Public Schools, Inc., Instructional Strategies Online Web site: http://olc.spsd.sk.ca/DE /PD/instr/

Accurately Assess Student Progress

Colorado Department of Education Exceptional Student Services Unit. (Fall 2004). *Grading and transcripts. Fast Facts: Secondary Transition Issues.* Retrieved September 29, 2006, from www.cde.state .co.us/cdesped/download/pdf/FF-Grading. pdf

Eggert, D. B. (2001, September). *Grading students with educational disabilities.* Paper presented at the 4th Annual Best Practices in Special and Regular Education Conference, Concord, New Hampshire. Retrieved September 29, 2006, from http://www.bridges4kids.org/articles/5-03/ Eggert9-01.html

Munk, D. (n.d.). *An introduction to grading.* Retrieved September 29, 2006, from http://www .specialconnections.ku.edu/cgi-bin/cgiwrap/specconn/main.php?cat = assessment&section = grading/main

Analyze Teaching/Teaching Styles

Patrick, H., Ryan, A. M., Anderman, L. H., Middleton, M., Linnenbrink, L., Hruda, L., Z., Edelin, K. C., Kaplan, A., & Midgley, C. (1997). *Observing Patterns of Adaptive Learning (OPAL): A protocol for classroom observations.* Ann Arbor: University of Michigan School of Education. Retrieved September 29, 2006, from www.umich.edu/ ~ pals/finalopal.pdf

Work With a Wide Range of Students

Strickland, C. A., & Tomlinson, C. A. (2005). *Differentiation in practice: A resource guide for differentiating curriculum, grades 9–12.* Arlington, VA: Association for Supervision and Curriculum Development.

Tomlinson, C. (1999). *The differentiated classroom: Responding to the needs of all learners.* Arlington, VA: Association for Supervision and Curriculum Development.

Knowledge of Course Content

Internet resources

Edsitement: The Best of the Humanities on the Web (National Endowment for the Humanities): http://edsitement.neh.gov/

PBS TeacherSource: http://www.pbs.org/teachersource/

PBS TeacherLine: http://teacherline.pbs.org/teacherline/welcome.cfm

varying instructional format. Both special and general educators can grow in their ability to embed instructional adaptations in daily lessons and expand their repertoire of instructional strategies to address the learning needs of all their students.

Murawski and Dieker wrote, "At the core of co-teaching is determining what instructional techniques will be most efficient and effective in helping all students meet academic standards" (2004, p. 55). Determining these instructional techniques is an ongoing process, made dynamic by the presence of two teachers. Keeping student needs, instructional effectiveness, and assessment of effectiveness at the center helps collaborative teams stay focused on improving student outcomes, together.

REFERENCES

Bradley, D. F., King-Sears, M. E., & Tessier-Switlick, D. M. (1997). *Teaching students in inclusive settings: From theory to practice.* Boston: Allyn & Bacon.

Friend, M., & Bursuck, W. D. (2002). *Including students with special needs: A practical guide for classroom teachers* (3rd ed.). Boston: Allyn & Bacon.

Friend, M., & Cook, L. (2002). *Interactions: Collaboration skills for school professionals* (4th ed.). New York: Longman.

Keefe, E. B., Moore, V., & Duff, F. (2004). The four "knows" of collaborative teaching. *TEACHING Exceptional Children, 36*(5), 36–41.

Murawski, W. W. (2003). *Co-teaching in the inclusive classroom: Working together to help all your students find success (grades 6–12).* Medina, WA: Institute for Educational Development.

Murawski, W. W., & Dieker, L. (2004). Tips and strategies for co-teaching at the secondary level. *TEACHING Exceptional Children, 36*(5), 52–58.

Murray, C. (2004). Clarifying collaborative roles in urban high schools: General educators' perspectives. *TEACHING Exceptional Children, 36*(5), 44–51.

National Education Association. (n.d.). *"Highly qualified" definition for special education teachers.* Retrieved September 28, 2006, from http://www.nea.org/lac/idea/highlyqualified.html

Wood, M. (1998). Whose job is it anyway? Educational roles in inclusion. *Exceptional Children, 64,* 181–195.

Originally published in *TEACHING Exceptional Children,* Vol. 39, No. 6, pp. 12–18.

7

10 Tips for Using Co-Planning Time More Efficiently

Wendy W. Murawski

Ms. Sheldon looked down at her notes from the co-teaching workshop she had just attended and sighed. Yes, she learned a lot about strategies for co-teaching and yes, she believed in the benefits. But was she the only one in the group who heard the presenter say in one breath that "co-planning is the most important component of co-teaching," followed by "finding time for co-planning is one of the most common barriers to effective co-teaching"? Ms. Sheldon thought, that was definitely her problem! She knew some great general education teachers who were willing and able to co-teach with her; the issue was little time to meet and co-plan with them. Was it even worth the attempt?

As Ms. Sheldon aptly noted, co-planning is both the most important and the most difficult component of co-teaching. Experts on co-teaching have repeatedly noted that without co-planning, teachers tend to teach without differentiation strategies and resort to a One Teach/One Support paradigm (Magiera & Zigmond, 2005; Murawski, 2010; Weiss & Lloyd, 2003). The premise of co-teaching rests on the shared expertise that special educator and classroom teacher collaboration brings to the instruction, not merely on having two adults in the classroom. Combine a general educator's knowledge of standards, curriculum, and content with a special educator's knowledge of differentiation strategies, a Title I teacher's knowledge of research-based reading strategies, or an English language specialist's knowledge, and the result can be impressive. Without time for sharing this expertise, teachers often teach a class the way they have always taught it and there is no "value added" by the second professional educator (Zigmond, 2006; Zigmond & Matta, 2004). Those teams are unable to answer the essential question of co-teaching: **How is what we are doing together substantively different, and better for students, than what one of us would do alone?**

This article provides 10 tips for how teachers can efficiently plan together, even with limited time. The more time teachers spend together, the better lessons can be, but unfortunately the reality is that few get that kind of time (Gurgur & Uzuner, 2010). In addition to general tips for planning, using a WHAT/HOW/WHO planning approach can help teachers maximize their planning time and still create a universally designed and differentiated lesson for an inclusive classroom.

#1: ESTABLISH A REGULAR TIME TO PLAN COLLABORATIVELY

Teachers never have enough time to do everything they need to do, and this includes planning for instruction. Having to meet with another teacher to plan is that much more complicated. For this reason, it is critical that co-teachers find a time that works for both of them and that they then hold that time sacrosanct for planning. Collaborating teachers must find at least a small amount of time (20 minutes minimum) once a week to meet. It's important that this planning time be held regularly; if it is scheduled as a regular occurrence and viewed as important, teachers can respond to requests accounting for the time in their schedule.

#2: SELECT AN APPROPRIATE ENVIRONMENT WITHOUT DISTRACTIONS

Classrooms are the typical place for teachers to meet and plan, but they are full of distractions. If you are going to use a classroom for planning, be sure to shut the door with a sign saying "Unavailable," turn off the phone, and sit together so you are not facing any other distracting elements. The school library, an open conference room, a testing office, the lunchroom or auditorium, or another teacher's empty classroom—these are all good alternative meeting spaces. For meetings before or after school or on weekends, coffee shops, restaurants, local libraries, parks, and each other's houses are all possibilities. Again, though, be aware of outside distractions such as noise, traffic, and interruptions.

#3: SAVE RAPPORT BUILDING FOR ANOTHER TIME

Co-teaching is frequently compared to a marriage (Kohler-Evans, 2006; Murawski, 2009, 2010), and it is definitely important for partners to get along and build rapport. However, too often planning sessions become gripe sessions or share sessions. Thirty minutes have passed and co-teachers have only discussed their personal anecdotes and stories. Planning sessions should be focused on planning. Keep rapport building and unrelated discussions for other times in order to maximize planning time.

#4: HAVE AN AGENDA AND SNACKS

At the beginning of every planning session, do a quick recap to determine what needs to be accomplished in the session. Having a checklist related to what needs to be accomplished helps the collaborators feel that there is a plan, and helps both teachers be on the same page in terms of discussion and time. In addition, if time runs out, teachers know what they need to discuss at a later time (either in person or by e-mail or phone conference). It is equally important to make sure your agenda identifies how long you have for this planning session. If one of you needs to leave in half an hour, note that right away so time is not wasted. Whatever time you've scheduled for this session, try to keep it to the time planned. If you typically plan to meet from 3:00 to 3:30 on Tuesdays and never leave the building until 5:30, after awhile one of you will become frustrated and disenchanted with planning. Instead, determine what you both think is a reasonable amount of time to plan and stick to it. If you keep finding yourselves running out of time, analyze your sessions to see if you have been chatting a lot or wasting time in other ways (e.g., getting materials you forgot, answering phones, both working on material that could have been divided). If you keep to your allotted time, you may find yourselves using time more efficiently and keeping to your agenda better.

The snacks suggestion is a practical one: Hungry teachers do not make the most agreeable or creative collaborators. Depending on when, where, and how long you are planning together, you may consider making sure there is food available, taking turns bringing snacks, or learning one another's coffee order.

#5: DETERMINE REGULAR ROLES AND RESPONSIBILITIES

Obviously, time is at a premium. Teachers know their own strengths and preferences in teaching, just as they know the areas in which they are not as strong. Save time by discussing these educational and personal characteristics in the beginning of your co-teaching relationship. There are certain tasks that happen frequently that you and your partner can identify as your individual roles, thereby saving time because you will not have to discuss them each time you plan. For example, one of you might always be responsible for coming up with warm-ups, while the other will be responsible for updating the homework board and web site. The more you can identify early on, the fewer things there will be to discuss at each planning session.

#6: DIVIDE AND CONQUER

Parity, or equality, is very important for successful collaboration (Friend & Cook, 2009). Both teachers need to feel they have an equal share in the planning, teaching, and assessing (Bouck, 2007; Murawski, 2009). If they don't, one may begin to feel like he or she is an overqualified aide, whereas the other feels the workload is not equitable and he or she is having to do most of the work (Bouck, 2007; Walther-Thomas, 1997). However, having parity does not mean that co-teachers need to do everything together. Once tasks are determined, they should be divided and attacked separately. Here is where using the regrouping approach to instruction (i.e., Parallel, Station, and Alternative Teaching) is beneficial. Teachers who are unfamiliar with the common approaches to co-instruction can refer to Table 1 for a quick overview. When students are divided into groups for instruction, not only does it reduce the student:teacher ratio; provide students with chunked content, brain breaks, and kinesthetic movement; and allow for easier checking for understanding and differentiation, but it also reduces the amount of planning teachers may need to do. Each teacher can plan a separate lesson and then repeat the content twice or more to a smaller group of students. Teachers certainly need to coordinate and discuss the standards, goals, and big picture of their instruction, but they do not need to spend time together going over the intricacies of each part of the lesson: This is where trust in one another comes in.

#7: KEEP A LIST OF INDIVIDUAL STUDENT CONCERNS

Kids are why we teach. Kids are the most important part of our job. Co-teachers definitely need to keep a focus on students and their learning (Friend, Cook, Hurley-Chamberlain, & Shamberger, 2010). However, you do not want to begin your planning session together by talking about individual students. This type of discussion will derail your planning; it is simply too easy to spend 45 minutes talking about how frustrating it is that Jake doesn't do anything in class, how amusing it is to watch Patrick's crush on Sandi, and how exciting it is that Quinn finally did his homework! Instead, keep a piece of paper handy to write down any individual student discussions you want to have at the end of your planning session. You will always find time to talk about students, even if it ends up happening as you are walking out to your cars together. What you do not want to have happen is that you start talking about the individual students and end up with no plan for what or how you are teaching tomorrow.

Table 1. Commonly Used Co-Teaching Approaches to Instruction

Co-Teaching Approach	Class Setup	Definition
One Teach/ One Support (OT/OS)	Whole class B A	One teacher is in front of the class leading instruction. The other is providing substantive support (e.g., collection or dissemination of papers, setting up labs, classroom management). Both are actively engaged.
Team teaching	Whole class A B	Both teachers are in front of the class, working together to provide instruction. This may take the form of debates, modeling information or note-taking, compare/contrast, or role-playing.
Parallel teaching	Regrouping A B	Each teacher takes half of the class in order to reduce student:teacher ratio. Instruction can occur in the same or a different setting. Groups may be doing the same content in the same way, same content in a different way, or different content.
Station teaching	Regrouping B A	Students are divided into three or more small, heterogeneous groups to go to stations or centers. Students rotate through multiple centers. Teachers can facilitate individual stations or circulate among all stations.
Alternative teaching	Regrouping A B	One teacher works with a large group of students, while the other works with a smaller group providing reteaching, preteaching, or enrichment as needed. The large group is not receiving new instruction during this time so that the small group can rejoin when finished.

Note. Adapted with permission from *Collaborate, Communicate, and Differentiate! How to Increase Student Learning in Today's Diverse Schools* by W. W. Murawski & S. A. Spencer, p. 97. Copyright 2011 by Corwin Press.

#8: BUILD IN REGULAR TIME FOR ASSESSMENT AND FEEDBACK

It is important that co-teachers communicate with one another openly, not just about the students and the content but also about their own teaching and interactions. Dieker (2008) recommends that teachers discuss their co-teaching progress at least monthly. Her *Co-Teaching Lesson Plan Book* provides questions to help teachers share honestly about what they think is working—and not working—in their co-teaching relationship. If you organize this type of check and dialogue early on by establishing it as something you will do as a matter of course, the conversation itself will be much less difficult because it will be expected.

#9: DOCUMENT YOUR PLANNING AND SAVE IT FOR FUTURE REFERENCE

Teachers are always planning. They pick up paper rulers when shopping to use in a math activity at school; they go on a date and think about how to tie the movie's plot into the theme they are teaching about next week; they find materials on a nature hike to use for a craft activity. The issue is not that teachers do not plan; it is merely that they do not always formally plan and that they do not have a lot of time to plan collaboratively. A major problem with planning between co-teachers is that it often occurs in an unorganized fashion. This results in a lesson that is either not well thought out, or one that ends up being great but cannot be duplicated because co-teachers are not really sure what they did. Because special educators often end up co-teaching with various partners in the same year, and general educators may very well have a different co-teaching partner next year than they have this year, much time would be saved if teachers did not keep recreating the wheel. When planning is done, be sure to keep a copy of the plan for future reference and improvement. In addition to regular planners and the *Co-Teaching Lesson Plan Book* (Dieker, 2008), the Co-Teaching Solutions System (www.coteachsolutions.com) software also provides ways for teachers to plan, e-mail their lessons to one another, add differentiation strategies, and spiral state standards.

#10: USE THE WHAT/HOW/WHO APPROACH

Now to the crux of the planning. You have a set schedule, agenda, nice nondistracting environment, the right mindset, identified roles, and some yummy snacks. You are ready to plan! The WHAT/HOW/WHO approach (Murawski & Spencer, 2011) is a way to quickly ensure that the lesson is state-standards-based, addresses grade-level content in accordance with pacing plans, and yet provides a good use of both teachers and their areas of expertise. The use of a timer as teachers plan each stage of the lesson (WHAT/HOW/WHO) will help keep the lesson focused, efficient, and effective.

Here's how it works: The first question discussed is "**WHAT** needs to be taught in this lesson?" The person who leads this conversation can be the teacher with the strongest background knowledge in the specific content. In approximately 5 minutes, the teacher should be able to identify the standards, objectives, timeframe, and big ideas of the lesson.

The next item discussed is "**How** will we teach this lesson in order to make sure it is universally accessible for all students?" Both co-teachers can equally take part in this conversation. During this part of the planning session, co-teachers should be able to identify how comfortable they are with the content, what approaches they could use, and what each of them will be responsible for prepping and/or teaching. Try to answer the "How" question in 7 to 15 minutes (depending on complexity of lesson, level of content knowledge of both teachers, rapport between teachers, etc.). After teaching together a while, this time requirement may decrease. Keep in mind that once teachers determine who is going to do what, they don't need to do all the specific in-depth planning together. For example, when using parallel teaching, one teacher can take the lead in planning a writing activity while the other teacher takes the lead in planning the comprehension activity. Students will be able to participate in both parts of the lesson but teachers only have to prepare half as much work.

The third, and final, item discussed is "**WHO** may need additional consideration in order to access this lesson?" The person who typically leads this conversation is the special education teacher or other special service provider (Title I, English-language teacher, gifted coordinator, etc.). In about 5 to 10 minutes, this special service provider should be able to identify who might struggle with the lesson, who might need certain adaptations or enrichment, and who might need to be contacted to come up with additional strategies for improving this lesson and its impact on all students (i.e., other adults). Table 2 provides additional questions to guide each of the three parts of the WHAT/HOW/WHO approach.

When teachers have worked together for awhile and are familiar with each other and the content, it is more likely they will need the lower end of the time range (i.e., 15 minutes). Teachers who are co-teaching for the first time or who are new to the content may need the upper end (e.g., 30 minutes). Either way, having a structure for planning will streamline the time and make it more effective.

Figure 1 demonstrates how the WHAT/HOW/WHO approach (Murawski & Spencer, 2011) has been used by co-teachers in planning and Figure 2 demonstrates how teachers might use the WHAT/HOW/WHO approach to guide more formal lesson planning. A blank template of Figure 2's co-planning form is available for free electronically at http://www.2TeachLLC.com/lessons.html. This format helps ensure documentation for future use.

Table 2. Questions to Guide Lesson Planning

WHAT	• What standard does the lesson address? • What objective does the lesson have? • What kind of timeframe do we have for instruction? • What are the "big ideas" and "essential questions" for this lesson?
HOW	• How comfortable do we both feel with the new content? • What co-teaching approach (i.e., Team, One Teach/One Support, Alternative, Station, or Parallel) will be most effective for the beginning of the lesson? • What co-teaching approach will be most effective for the middle of the lesson? • What co-teaching approach will be most effective for the end of the lesson? • Based on the co-teaching approaches selected, what are each teacher's responsibilities for planning, bringing in materials, implementing, and assessing?
WHO	• Who might struggle behaviorally, socially, or academically with aspects of the lesson? • Who needs accommodations or modifications or adapted materials? • What additional types of differentiation strategies would make the lesson more interesting, motivating, enriching, or accessible for all learners? • Who else may need to be included in helping make the lesson accessible (e.g., speech teacher, occupational therapist, parent, Braille teacher)?

FINAL THOUGHTS

Time is a definite issue for all teachers and this issue is compounded for those who are collaborating in support of children with special needs. The WHAT/HOW/WHO approach (Murawski & Spencer, 2011) helps structure lesson planning for co-teachers struggling with this issue. Dieker's research (2001) found that veteran co-teachers can effectively plan lessons in only 10 minutes. The key word here, however, is "veteran." Once a team has been together for awhile, they naturally require much less time as they only need to tweak lessons already crafted. Unfortunately, most co-teachers do not feel that they have sufficient time to co-plan in the first place. Using these 10 tips for co-planning will help make the most of the little time teachers have and will result in better, more individualized and differentiated lessons for the co-taught inclusive classroom.

Figure 1. Example of What/How/Who Approach to Lesson Planning

WHAT/HOW/WHO Co-Planning Form		
General educator: **Rick G.**		Special service provider: **Marcia R.**
Lesson date: **October 3**		Subject/grade: **English 8th**
WHAT (5 minutes)	Standard	LA.1.2.1. Understand the common features of a variety of literary forms.
	Objective	Students will be able to identify and create haiku & acrostic poems.
	Big idea (all need to know)	There are different types of poems.
	Essential question (all can answer)	Do poems have to rhyme?
	Timeframe for lesson	55-minute period; only 1 period available for this.
How (7–15 minutes)	Comfort Level with Content	Both comfortable, but Marcia prefers acrostics
	Beginning (approach & description)	OT/OS: R take roll as M reads two poems (1 acrostic; 1 haiku) as "hook"; students briefly discuss similarities and differences (10 minutes)
	Middle (approach & description)	Parallel: R take ½ class and teach haiku; M take ½ and teach acrostics; switch & repeat after 15 minutes; total 32 minutes w/ 2-minute transition time
	End (approach & description)	Alternative: R has large group do Ticket Out the Door (TOTD) with poems using Cloze procedure; M keeps small group who needs more time to finish haiku/acrostic poems (10 minutes)
	Special ed responsibilities for preparation/instruction	Copy model poems; make accommodations to poems & TOTD; try to get poems in Spanish & Braille
	General ed responsibilities for preparation/instruction	Identify poems for beginning of class; identify model poems for Marcia to copy; create TOTD poem for end; consider higher level questions for Gifted students
WHO (5 minutes)	Needs behavioral adaptions?	Remind Javon & Tim about transition & group behavior; sit Javon near teacher in both groups
	Needs social adaptations?	Remind Ryan how to ask for help & sit near a friend
	Needs physical adaptations?	Have large print version available for Brenda
	Needs instructional adaptations?	Have model poems & Cloze procedure poems available; let Kiernan write poems about Bionicles to keep interest; challenge Oliver by asking him to rhyme his acrostics & use multiple adjectives in haiku; provide Spanish version for Javier & Lupe
	Contact for additional input	Give poems to Ms. H for Braille translation; ask Mr. Valdez about SDAIE strategies/suggestions
	Implementing/ensuring adaptations	R - do reminders during beginning (OT/OS), come up with challenging questions, and have model problems ready for Marcia M - do large print copies, contact Mr. V for SDAIE and Ms. H for Braille

Note. OT/OS = One Teach/One Support. SDAIE = specially designed academic instruction.

Figure 2. Sample Co-Planned Lesson

General Educator: __Rick G.__   Special Service Provider: __Marcia R.__

Step 1:
The first section is done during the WHAT part of the lesson (approximately 5 minutes)

Co-Teaching Lesson Plan

Subject Area: __Language Arts__

Grade level: __8th__

Content Standard: __LA.1.2.1. The student understands the common features of a variety of literary forms__

Lesson Objective: __Students will be able to identify & create a haiku and acrostic poem.__

Essential Questions: __Do poems have to rhyme? Big Idea: There are different types of poems.__

Key Vocabulary: __Poem, haiku, acrostic, rhyme__

Pre-Assessment: __Day before – Do Know-Want to Know-Learned (KWL) about poems to see who already knows acrostics/haiku__

Materials: __Model poems of haiku & acrostics; ticket out the door w/Cloze; large print poems for Brenda; Braille version of poems for Quinn; put poems & homework on web site; powerpoints & handouts; magnetic letters & magnetic cookie sheets; dry erase boards & markers__

Lesson	Co-Teaching Approach (can select more than one)	Time	General Education Teacher	Special Service Provider	Considerations (may include adaptations, differentiation, accommodations, and student-specific needs)
Beginning: (may include: Opening; Warm Up; Review; Anticipatory Set)	☑ One Teach, One Support ☐ Parallel ☐ Alternative ☐ Station ☐ Team	10 minutes	Take roll / Get materials prepared / Pass out cards with "Haiku" or "Acrostic" so students know which group to go to first / Talk to students who need proactive reminders	Read 2 poems (haiku, acrostic) / Lead students in oral discussion of similarities & differences between poems	Remind Javon & Tim about transition & group behavior; remind Ryan how to ask for help & sit near friend during group work; have copies of poems available for students to look at (on overhead, large copy); ask higher order questions of Oliver
Middle: (may include: Instruction; Checking for Understanding; Independent or Group Practice)	☐ One Teach, One Support ☑ Parallel ☐ Alternative ☐ Station ☐ Team	32 minutes (15 per group + 2 minute switch)	Take ½ class and teach haiku using powerpoint and examples (good for visual/auditory learners); students can use dry erase boards or paper as desired / Switch after 15 minutes and repeat	Take ½ class and teach acrostics using magnetic letters & cookie sheets (good for kinesthetic learners) / Switch after 15 min and repeat	Let Kiernan write poems about Bionicles to keep interest; challenge Oliver by asking him to rhyme his acrostics & use multiple adjectives in haiku; have example poems available for all students to see; use mnemonics for remembering differences; have dry erase markers and boards available for students like Amy who prefer to write and erase multiple times before committing to paper
End: (may include: Closing; Assessments; Extension of the Lesson)	☐ One Teach, One Support ☐ Parallel ☑ Alternative ☐ Station ☐ Team	10 minutes	Have large group do "Ticket out the Door" by completing poems using Cloze procedure / Remind students to write down homework from board into their planners	Work with small group of students who need more time or assistance in understanding Haiku & Acrostics / Remind students to write down homework from board into their planners	During transition to large group, both teachers can decide who needs extra time in small group. Small group can meet at back table. Have multiple copies of Cloze versions of Ticket out the Door to ensure differentiation; allow Oliver, Kiernan, Amy, and others who want to create poems from scratch if desired; adapt level of homework based on individual need

Step 2: The middle section is done during the HOW part of the lesson (approximately 7 to 15 minutes)

Step 3: The considerations section is last and is done during the WHO part of the lesson (approximately 5 minutes)

Note. Adapted with permission from http://www.2TeachLLC.com/lessons.html. A free co-teaching lesson plan template is available at www.2TeachLLC.com.

REFERENCES

Bouck, E. C. (2007). Co-teaching . . . Not just a textbook term: Implications for practice. *Preventing School Failure, 51*(2), 46–51. http://dx.doi.org/10.3200/PSFL.51.2.46-51

Dieker, L. A. (2001). What are the characteristics of "effective" middle and high school co-taught teams? *Preventing School Failure, 46*(1), 14–25. http://dx.doi.org/10.1080/10459880109603339

Dieker, L. A. (2008). *Co-teaching lesson plan book.* Whitefish Bay, WI: Knowledge by Design.

Friend, M., & Cook, L. (2009). *Interactions: Collaboration skills for school professionals* (6th ed.). Boston, MA: Allyn & Bacon.

Friend, M., Cook, L., Hurley-Chamberlain, D., & Shamberger, C. (2010). Co-teaching: An illustration of the complexity of collaboration in special education. *Journal of Educational and Psychological Consultation, 20,* 9–27. http://dx.doi.org/10.1080/10474410903535380

Gurgur, H., & Uzuner, Y. (2010). A phenomenological analysis of the views on co-teaching applications in the inclusion classroom. *Educational Sciences: Theory and Practice, 10*(1), 311–331.

Kohler-Evans, P. (2006). Co-teaching: How to make this marriage work in front of the kids. *Education, 127,* 260–264.

Magiera, K., & Zigmond, N. (2005). Co-teaching in middle school classrooms under routine conditions: Does the instructional experience differ for students with disabilities in co-taught and solo-taught classes? *Learning Disabilities Research & Practice, 20,* 79–85. http://dx.doi.org/10.1111/j.1540-5826.2005.00123.x

Murawski, W. W. (2009). *Collaborative teaching in secondary schools: Making the co-teaching marriage work!* Thousand Oaks, CA: Corwin Press.

Murawski, W. W. (2010). *Collaborative teaching in elementary schools: Making the co-teaching marriage work!* Thousand Oaks, CA: Corwin Press.

Murawski, W. W., & Spencer, S. A. (2011). *Collaborate, communicate, and differentiate! How to increase student learning in today's diverse schools.* Thousand Oaks, CA: Corwin Press.

Walther-Thomas, C. S. (1997). Coteaching experiences: The benefits and problems that teachers and principals report over time. *Journal of Learning Disabilities, 30,* 395–407. http://dx.doi.org/10.1177/002221949703000406

Weiss, M. P., & Lloyd, J. (2003). Conditions for co-teaching: Lessons from a case study. *Teacher Education and Special Education, 26,* 27–41. http://dx.doi.org/10.1177/088840640302600104

Zigmond, N. (2006). Reading and writing in co-taught secondary school social studies classrooms: A reality check. *Reading and Writing Quarterly, 22,* 249–267. http://dx.doi.org/10.1080/10573560500455711

Zigmond, N., & Matta, D. (2004). Value added of the special education teacher in secondary school co-taught classes. In T. E. Scruggs & M. A. Mastropieri (Eds.), *Advances in learning and behavioral disabilities.* (pp. 55–76). Greenwich, CT: JAI Press.

The author would like to acknowledge the many co-teachers nationally who continue to collaborate daily to help all students succeed—even when they aren't given additional time to do so.

Originally published in *TEACHING Exceptional Children,* Vol. 44, No. 4, pp. 8–15.

8

Don't Give Up!
Practical Strategies for
Challenging Collaborations

Sharon Cramer and Jan Stivers

Lindsey T., third year special education consulting teacher,
Pine View Elementary School:

"Never again! On Friday, I talked to Samantha about the problems my students were having with the math homework she assigns. She promised that she would have a few options for us to discuss after the weekend. When I reminded her this morning, she didn't even look guilty about forgetting. Her face was a total blank, and she said, 'Lindsey, you'll have to remind me—did I promise you something?' She didn't even remember our conversation! I've tried so many times, and nothing works. Why do I bother?"

Samantha K., first year teacher, Pine View Elementary School:

"I spent all weekend trying to come up with something for Lindsey, but I couldn't think of anything. I felt more and more frustrated. But when she came up to me today, I couldn't admit that I didn't have any ideas. It was easier to play dumb. How are we going to make this collaboration work?"

The teachers in this situation are not able to admit they are having problems, and they are not alone. People faced with collaboration challenges are often reluctant to be honest about problems because in many schools collaboration is a norm (e.g., Burnett & Peters-Johnson, 2004; Villa & Thousand, 2005). But whereas most special educators are intuitively skilled at working with others, "problematic professional encounters are *inevitable* barriers that will appear occasionally in the life of every special educator" (Cramer, 2006, p. 6). This article draws on the professional literature in education and in business management (see box "What Does the Literature Say About Teacher Collaboration?"), as well as on the experiences of hundreds of teachers, to offer evidence-based strategies for addressing challenges in teacher collaborations.

How Can I Collaborate With a Teacher Whose Style Is Very Different From Mine?

Situation: I'm a new consultant teacher, and think I was hired partly because I'm very outgoing. This has worked well with Robert; we seem to complement each other, and we get a lot done in the classroom. But Jocelyn, the other teacher with whom I collaborate, is very reserved. I doubt that the two of us are ever going to really see things the same way. I'm afraid that my enthusiasm is putting her off; as a result I become self-conscious. I don't like the passive role I've begun to take within the class, but don't know how to turn things around.

Good news! The recent experience of collaborating teachers (e.g., Mastropieri et al., 2005) and the long history of teams in the business world (e.g., Drucker, 1994) point to two important truths:

1. You can collaborate effectively with people who are quite different from you.
2. No single collaborative approach works for everyone.

Rather than think about the "right" or "wrong" way to collaborate, consider instead what you can do to make effective collaboration easier. Roger Fisher has helped negotiators all over the world develop a win-win approach in which they find common ground and use it to create an outcome that is acceptable to both parties (Fisher, Ury, & Patton, 1991). Fisher and his colleagues would recommend that you shift your thinking: view adjustments in your approach to collaboration not as compromises you must make in your teaching style but as steps you are willing to take to achieve your overall goal of working well together. Consider, too, that in teaching as in management, many models exist for effective collaboration (Bauwens & Hourcade, 2003; Drucker, 1994; Friend & Cook, 2007). The models and strategies you are using successfully in one class may not work in another, but with time and effort you can find strategies that will work in the new setting. Finding collaborative models that work for each of the settings in which you teach is vitally important. Otherwise, you risk settling into a passive role or serving primarily as a teacher assistant, and fail to make full use of the special educator's professional knowledge and skills—and without doubt, your students will lose out.

What Does the Literature Say About Teacher Collaboration?

Collaboration is no longer just an ingredient in school life but an essential feature (Burnett & Peters-Johnson, 2004; Villa & Thousand, 2005.) It is central to progressive educational reform efforts, according to Mohr and Dichter (2001), because "authentic learning requires an authentic learning community" (p. 747). It is essential to the professional growth that characterizes responsive schools; as Miller, Ray, Dove, & Kenreich (2000) say, "To be able to share insights and work with other colleagues helps to break the isolation and keep us alive as educators" (p. 146). Caron and McLaughlin (2002) identify the presence of a "collaborative culture" as an indicator of an excellent school while noting that collaborative strategies that prove to be effective vary from classroom to classroom. Research projects examining collaboration in the context of early childhood education (e.g., Pianta, Kraft-Sayre, Rimm-Kaufman, Gercke, & Higgins, 2001), elementary education (e.g., Welch, 2000), and secondary settings (e.g., Bouck, 2005) illustrate the variations that can be found in the extended interactions between general and special educators. Collaboration has the potential to make those interactions productive and satisfying for all involved, to the benefit of the students (Idol, 2006).

As the number of special needs students receiving their education in inclusive settings increases, there will be higher expectations for collaboration among special educators, general educators, related service personnel, and paraprofessionals (Gerlach, 2005). Collaboration will likely soon be a fact of life for all those who work with students with disabilities. According to Fisher, Frey, and Thousand (2003), the ability to collaborate is "fundamental" for special educators; they add, "Successful special educators are masters of collaboration" (p. 46). Fortunately, the skills needed for successful collaboration can be learned (Cramer, 2006; Stivers, Lavoie, Perner, & Kinn, 2003), and studies of collaborating teachers have found that they generally evaluate their collaborative skills positively and regard their relationships with their teaching partners as satisfying (e.g., Idol, 2006; Salend & Johansen, 1997).

However, even intelligent and well-intentioned teachers, diligently trying to work together, at times may find that genuine collaboration eludes them. Stumbling blocks to collaboration are both conceptual and pragmatic; they include such factors as a climate of competition rather than cooperation; a lack of clarity about underlying values and beliefs; and inadequate administrative support, planning time, and opportunities for professional development in collaborative skills (Leonard & Leonard, 2003). Although more experienced teachers are significantly more likely to refer to collaboration as a strategy that helps enhance student outcomes (Stough & Palmer, 2001; Stough, Palmer, & Sharp, 2001), experience alone is insufficient to ensure success (Trent, 1998). Teachers can take actions to strengthen their collaborative relationships (Stivers, in press), and in the process they can also change their ways of thinking about their work, and come to value collaboration (Ripley, 1998) for themselves and their students.

Sometimes what appear to be differences in teaching styles are in fact differences in verbal and nonverbal communication styles. To broaden your repertoire of communication skills and to turn your situation into a learning opportunity, develop a strategic approach to listening. Covey's (1989) recommendation is to learn to "listen with the intent to *understand*. . . . Empathic (from empathy) listening gets inside another person's frame of reference. You look out through it, you see the world the way they see the world, you understand their paradigm, you understand how they feel" (p. 240). Thus, instead of looking at your situation as indentured servitude with someone you did not choose to partner with, you can use the working relationship as a laboratory for learning to listen. Putting yourself in charge of a goal you select enables you to give up the feeling that you are adjusting unnecessarily.

Of course you will encounter situations in which differences in teaching or communication styles cannot fully explain your lack of compatibility with another teacher. As Sandi Kolk, assistant superintendent in the Lakeland (NY) Central School District, explains in Stivers (in press), co-teachers and collaborating teachers are not always similar in personality or temperament. Those working relationships have built-in limitations that can be an advantage: "Your co-teacher may not be a person you'd choose to spend time with outside of school. That's okay. This is a professional relationship, and it succeeds when both parties behave professionally."

Although you may presume that little can be accomplished if only one person is invested in making the collaborative relationship more effective, that outcome is not necessarily true. Cramer (2006) documents the amazing progress that can be made by teachers who make a commitment to working with another professional in a different way, even if they must do so alone. She explains, "Each relationship develops its own kind of balance. Visualize it as a teeter-totter. When both people stay in the same positions in relation to each other, there is little likelihood of change. When one moves, both are influenced" (p. 9).

Ideally, the change results in new behaviors; sometimes, though, only changes in attitude result. But even small attitudinal changes can make palpable differences. The example that follows, adapted from teacher reports, is typical:

When I started to work on improving our relationship, I decided to pick a problem I faced with my co-teacher all the time. She loves to complain about the school administration. It makes me very uncomfortable; especially since I think her criticisms are exaggerated and sometimes unfair. But I didn't want to do or say anything to alienate her, because she really is a good teacher for my students. As I learned more about collaboration, I realized that I couldn't control her complaining, but I could control my response to it. I learned to avoid responding to her complaints, and as a result our joint prep period each day is less stressful for me. To an outside observer it would look as if nothing has changed; she still complains every day. The change is that I don't let it get to me anymore. I just accept it as part of her style, something I'm willing to accommodate in the interest of preserving a relationship that serves my students well. It was important for me to learn that we can work together, even if we are not completely compatible.

Making the changes you can make—even if they are changes only in your outlook—can be empowering. Teachers who can let go of negative self-talk or disappointment in the failures of others may find they have more energy for constructive pursuits.

How Long Does Change Take?

Situation: I know that all things take time, but it is almost the end of the school year! I still haven't seen any change in the working relationships I've tried to establish with my general education colleagues. Our interactions are cordial, even friendly—but they are not the collaborations I had hoped for.

First, realize that the process of change is gradual, not sudden. Instead of seeing the process as a light switch, consider it to be more like a dimmer. In a year-long study, Phillips, Sapona, and Lubic (1995) trained, interviewed, and observed six general education teachers and the four special education teachers with whom they co-taught. At the end of the year, the teachers advised, "be prepared to 'put in time' getting to know your teaching partner; this phase cannot be rushed. It takes time to learn about each other's styles and preferences" (p. 269). This measured approach may be challenging for teachers who have two qualities that Bauwens and Hourcade (2003) identify as important for effective collaboration: an inner pressure to achieve results and a high level of confidence in their own abilities. But Bauwens and Hourcade emphasize two other equally important elements: respect for, and trust in, one's partners and a tolerance of failure and mistakes while seeking results.

Second, help yourself by thinking about your effort as similar to other change initiatives. Co-teaching is a popular form of teacher collaboration that requires each partner to make changes and accommodations; researchers who have investigated the development of co-teaching relationships (e.g., Gately & Gately, 2001; Phillips et al., 1995) have observed that the changes typically proceed in stages. They note that in the early stages, co-teachers may feel uncertain and perhaps anxious; however, even collaborations that have a slow start can develop into satisfying professional relationships. Bridges (2003) provides a model in which the process of change involves letting go of old ways and dealing with the uncertainty of trying out new behaviors before new routines can be established.

To understand the challenges of change, start by looking at how connected we are to our routines and habits. If you try to change even simple things (such as putting your socks on in reverse order, driving to work via a different route, taking public transportation to a new location), you will see that you have to concentrate on these new approaches. You cannot change even uncomplicated habits such as these without focus and effort. Next consider the challenges faced by your general education colleagues when you ask them to modify complex instructional procedures they have spent years perfecting. Such modifications will require not only skill and willpower but patience and dedication on the part of all involved. Make sure that you are realistic about any initiative you undertake, so that you do not become frustrated.

STRATEGIES FOR IMPLEMENTING CHANGE

Instead of "watching the clock" and waiting for other people to change their ways, teach yourself to focus on the aspects of your working relationships that are under your control. Blanchard, Bowles, Carew, and Parisi-Carew (2000) wrote a popular trade book in which concepts about change are incorporated into a story about a fifth-grade ice hockey team. The difficulties adults and boys in the story have are very relevant to teachers. As team members learn to focus on achieving individual goals to advance their teamwork skills, they stop blaming one another and make progress. You can apply this concept to your collaborative relationships. Instead of trying to get other teachers to understand you, shift your focus to learning more about them. As you begin to understand and value what is important to the other teachers, you will find that you have stopped waiting. To help you manage the change process, and your responses to it, consider using one of these strategies:

- *Establish a personal collaboration resource network.* Cramer (2006) provides suggestions for selecting people whose perspective on your collaborative situation will help you gain new insights. Some may be people who work in your school setting, whereas others may know little about the specifics of your school situation but know you very well. The latter individuals may be able to give you useful feedback about your collaborative strengths and advice about how to build on your prior experiences. This "network" of individuals may not ever meet face to face. Think of them as a virtual group that can help you reconsider your goals and the progress you are making toward achieving them. Use the prompts in Figure 1 to identify individuals who might be invited to participate in your network.

- *Create and participate in collaborative communities.* Walther-Thomas, Korinek, and McLaughlin (1999) go a step further than a network to assist you in developing a deeper understanding of your collaborative relationships. They suggest creating communities that "support ongoing teamwork in many ways, [such as] teacher assistance teams and various types of school-improvement committees" (p. 3). By joining some of the schoolwide initiatives, you may find that your focus has shifted away from what you cannot change to what you can contribute.

Figure 1. Establishing a Collaboration Resource Network

Directions: Next to each prompt, list as many names as come to mind. Think beyond the people with whom you usually interact at school; consider using e-mail or telephone to communicate with resource people who are not nearby, or who have busy schedules.

A person who works at your school, who could maintain your confidences

_____
_____

A person whom you have known for a long time, who can make you laugh

_____
_____

A person who has a good perspective on things

_____
_____

A person who is an effective problem solver

_____
_____

A person with whom you lost touch, with whom you'd like to reconnect

_____
_____

A professor who had good insights about either course content or about how to assist you in doing your coursework

_____
_____

A friend with whom you talk regularly about work

_____
_____

From all the people you have selected, pick three or four with whom you would be able to communicate a few times during the next few months as you focus on improving your collaborative relationship. Explain what you are trying to accomplish, and incorporate each person's advice into your collaboration efforts.

Adapted from S. F. Cramer, *The Special Educator's Guide to Collaboration*, pp. 154–155, copyright 2006 by Corwin Press. Reprinted by permission of the publisher.

Serving as part of a mentoring network for new teachers at your school can be fulfilling. Stivers (in press) suggests that "explaining your beliefs and practices [to new co-teaching pairs] can help you think more critically about the . . . decisions you make." Mandel (2006) emphasizes the importance of helping new teachers: "New teachers aren't thinking about raising scores on the standardized test in May; they are more concerned about how to get through fifth period tomorrow. First year teachers have one basic goal—survival" (p. 66). Working with first-year teachers provides an invaluable service that also can help you realize how far you have come as a teacher, while strengthening your connection to your school community.

- *Keep track of your progress so that you do not become discouraged.* Use any method that works for you to help you see how things are shifting. It is easy to miss some of the changes you are making.
  - *Objective data.* In monitoring objective data (e.g., number of interactions over the course of a week or the proportion of substantive interactions to superficial exchanges), you may find that more is happening than you thought. You can also look for patterns that can help you focus your efforts. For example, does face-to-face interaction work better than e-mail? Is before school better than after?
  - *Subjective data.* If you can develop criteria for subjective measures, you can give yourself credit for the subtle changes you are making in your behavior. Consider, for example, rating your level of confidence during planned discussions, or awarding "quality points" for initiating spontaneous interactions or forgiving yourself and others for minor mistakes.

Becoming a teacher who can effectively collaborate requires that you keep track of what you are doing that is effective, as well as what you need to modify. Learning how to judge your progress accurately is a valuable skill and one that can help you empathize with your students.

How Can I Talk to My Colleagues About New Ideas for Teaching?

Situation: I've been a special education consulting teacher at the same school for several years. I've got good working relationships with several teachers, and my students are learning. Yet I know things could be better. Whenever I bring up a new idea from a workshop or article, I get no response. It seems as if I can talk to my colleagues about anything except changing the way we do things.

It may help to take a step back to see your collaborative relationship within the broader context of your school and district. Your concerns are probably not unique to your own collaborative relationships. You may have more success if you find ways to incorporate your ideas into ongoing professional development activities within your school, district, or professional organization. Here are some ways to get started:

- The next time your school needs to send a teacher to a mandatory workshop, such as training for scoring standardized tests, volunteer to be the one to attend and report back to others about what you have learned. This expertise gives you legitimacy for sharing ideas.
- Delve into the professional literature of your general education colleagues. As Mason, Thormann, O'Connell, and Behrmann (2004) recommend, "scan their [W]eb sites, read some of their association reports, and keep track of articles that are published in at least some of their journals" (p. 227). You are likely to find points of intersection between your concerns

and theirs; if not, the discovery process in itself could give you things to discuss.

- Attend a professional development workshop with one of your general education colleagues, as Stivers (in press) advises. Together, you may find ways to incorporate what you have heard at the workshop into activities at your school.

- Join the professional development or superintendent's day committee in your school or district. Through the use of needs assessments and interest surveys, you can find topics of interest to the teachers with whom you work. Once plans are under way for the next professional development day, establish a Web site (by working with the technology-proficient people in your district) and build excitement about the event by posting information about speakers and providing links to online reference materials that are relevant to both general and special educators. As a follow-up to the professional development event, establish a discussion board so that interested teachers and other professionals can discuss how they are using the workshop content. Those individuals who are interested in pursuing use of the content could become a resource group throughout the school year.

Do not stop being intrigued with the possibilities of integrating relevant content into conversations and events in your school. Make sure that your sharing is timely and well connected to interests of others in your school.

FINAL THOUGHTS

Collaborative relationships can be a rich source of professional and personal growth, well worth the investment of time and effort that may be needed to nurture them. As with all human relationships, things will not always go smoothly. When difficulties arise, teachers can examine their assumptions and practices, and make adjustments that enable progress to take place. There are no quick fixes; addressing challenges in collaborative relationships takes reflection, energy, and persistence. However, even in imperfect situations, teachers who persevere can find new, gratifying, and mutually satisfying ways to work with others.

REFERENCES

Bauwens, J., & Hourcade, J. J. (2003). *Cooperative teaching: Rebuilding the schoolhouse for all students* (2nd ed.). Austin, TX: Pro-Ed.

Blanchard, K., Bowles, S. M., Carew, D., & Parisi-Carew, E. (2000). *High five: The magic of working together.* New York: William Morrow.

Bouck, E. C. (2005). Secondary special educators: Perspectives of preservice preparation and satisfaction. *Teacher Education and Special Education, 28*(2), 125–139.

Bridges, W. (2003). *Managing transitions: Making the most of change.* Cambridge, MA: DaCapo Press, Perseus Books Group.

Burnett, J., & Peters-Johnson, C. (Eds.). (2004). *Thriving as a special educator: Balancing your practices and your ideals.* Alexandria, VA: Council for Exceptional Children.

Caron, E. A., & McLaughlin, M. J. (2002). Indicators of Beacons of Excellence Schools: What do they tell us about collaborative practices? *Journal of Educational and Psychological Consultation, 13*(4), 285–313.

Covey, S. R. (1989). *The seven habits of highly effective people: Powerful lessons in personal change.* New York: Simon & Schuster.

Cramer, S. F. (2006). *The special educator's guide to collaboration.* Thousand Oaks, CA: Corwin Press.

Drucker, P. F. (1994, November). The age of social transformation. *The Atlantic Monthly, 274,* 53–80.

Fisher, D., Frey, N., & Thousand, J. (2003). What do special educators need to know and be prepared to do for inclusive schooling to work? *Teacher Education and Special Education, 26*(1), 42–50.

Fisher, R., Ury, W., & Patton, B. (1991). *Getting to yes: Negotiating without giving in.* (2nd ed.). New York: Penguin Books.

Friend, M., & Cook, L. (2007). *Interactions: Collaboration skills for school professionals.* (5th ed.). Boston: Allyn & Bacon.

Gately, S. E., & Gately. F. J. (2001). Understanding coteaching components. *TEACHING Exceptional Children, 33*(4), 40–47.

Gerlach, K. (2005). *The paraeducator and teacher team: Strategies for success.* Seattle: Pacific Training Associates.

Individuals With Disabilities Education Act 2004 20 U.S.C. §§ 1400 et. seq.

Idol, L. (2006). Toward inclusion of special education students in general education. *Remedial and Special Education, 27*(2), 77–94.

Leonard, L., & Leonard, P. (2003, September 17). The continuing trouble with collaboration: Teachers talk. Current Issues in Education 6(15). Retrieved June 5, 2006, from http://cie.ed.asu.edu/volume6/number15/

Mandel, S. (2006). What new teachers really need. *Educational Leadership, 63*(6), 66–69.

Mason, C., Thormann, M. S., O'Connell, M., & Behrmann, J. (2004). Priority issues reflected in general and special education association journals. *Exceptional Children, 70,* 215–229.

Mastropieri, M. A., Scruggs, T. E., Graetz, J., Norland, J., Gardizi, W., & McDuffie, K. (2005). Case studies in co-teaching in the content areas: Successes, failures, and challenges. *Intervention in School and Clinic, 40*(5), 260–270.

Miller, S. L., Ray, S., Dove, T., & Kenreich, T. (2000). Perspectives on personal professional development. In M. Johnston, P. Brosnan, D. Cramer, & T. Dove (Eds.), *Collaborative reform and other improbable dreams* (pp. 141–151). Albany: State University of New York Press.

Mohr, N., & Dichter, A. 2001. Building a learning organization. *Phi Delta Kappan, 82*(10), 744–747.

Phillips, C., Sapona, R. H., & Lubic, B. L. (1995). Developing partnerships in inclusive education: One school's approach. *Intervention in School and Clinic, 30*(5), 262–272.

Pianta, R. C., Kraft-Sayre, M., Rimm-Kaufman, S., Gercke, N., & Higgins, T. (2001). Collaboration in building partnerships between families and schools: The

National Center for Early Development and Learning's Kindergarten Transition Intervention. *Early Childhood Research Quarterly, 16*(1), 117–132.

Ripley, S. (1998). Teaching strategies: Collaboration between general and special education teachers. *Journal of Early Education and Family Review, 5*(4), 16–20.

Salend, S. J., & Johansen, M. (1997). Cooperative teaching: The voices of two teachers. *Remedial and Special Education, 18*(1), 3–11.

Stivers, J. (in press). Twenty ways to strengthen your co-teaching relationship. *Intervention in School and Clinic.*

Stivers, J., Lavoie, J., Perner, D., & Kinn, B. (2003, October.) *Human relations skills for inclusive education.* Paper presented at the annual conference of the Northeastern Educational Research Association, Kerhonkson, NY.

Stough, L. M., & Palmer, D. J. (2001, April). *Teacher reflection: How effective special educators differ from novices.* Paper presented at the annual Council for Exceptional Children conference, Kansas City, MO. (ERIC Document Reproduction Service No. ED463279)

Stough, L. M., Palmer, D. J., & Sharp, A. N. (2001, February). *Teachers' reflections on special education students' cognition.* Paper presented at the annual meeting of the Southwest Educational Research Association, New Orleans, LA. (ERIC Document Reproduction Service No. ED452626)

Trent, S. C. (1998). False starts and other dilemmas of a secondary general education collaborative teacher: A case study. *Journal of Learning Disabilities, 31*(5), 503–513.

Villa, R. A., & Thousand, J. S. (2005). *Creating an inclusive school.* (2nd ed.). Alexandria, VA: Association for Supervision and Curriculum Development.

Walther-Thomas, C., Korinek, L., & McLaughlin, V. L. (1999). Collaboration to support students' success. *Focus on Exceptional Children, 32*(3), 1–18.

Welch, M. (2000). Descriptive analysis of team teaching in two elementary classrooms: A formative experimental approach. *Remedial and Special Education, 21*(6), 366–376.

Originally published in *TEACHING Exceptional Children,* Vol. 39, No. 6, pp. 6–11.

9

"Survivors" or "Friends"? A Framework for Assessing Effective Collaboration

Kathryn C. Wiggins and Sharon J. Damore

We live in a fast-paced time that demands multitasking and a growing sensitivity to world issues. Communication, collaboration, and cooperation are factors that can contribute to effective performance in this age, regardless of whether one is referring to business deals, political campaigns, the protection of the environment, or the education of children. Ever-growing demands on classroom teachers have made collaboration among professional educators a must. Meeting the needs of an increasingly diverse student population is a daunting task, one that research shows can be done best collaboratively (McLeskey & Waldron, 2002; Walther-Thomas, Korinek, McLaughlin, & Williams, 2002).

Increasing technological connections is beneficial; but we need interpersonal connectivity, where people form meaningful connections through idea-sharing networks (Schmitz, Baber, & Brown, 2000). All too often, unfortunately, attempts at a collaboration process create an environment where the participants view themselves as survivors rather than friends and professional colleagues. This psychological "short" in the human collaboration connection results in ineffectiveness.

Within our model, we define collaboration as a system of planned cooperative activities where general educators and special educators share roles and responsibilities for student learning. We have found certain elements that must be present if collaboration between educators is to be productive and effective. We have identified these elements to include positive attitude, team process, professional development, leadership, resources, and benefits (see Figure 1).

ASSESSMENT FRAMEWORK

We created an assessment framework that characterizes levels of development across our six key elements of collaboration. Using our rubric and identifying developmental levels of each of the elements, a school can determine its strengths and target its energies and resources for improvement. A completed checklist, based on the "Elements of Collaboration Rubric," enables a school to complete an "Action Plan" to guide and monitor future efforts to improve collaboration. The use of a rubric generally requires some training to ensure common understanding and interpretation of terms as well as reliability of use. Let's examine each element in more detail.

Positive Attitude

There is a developmental continuum to the process of establishing professional relationships leading to effective collaboration where the roles of the participants are clear and individuals have a chance to strengthen relationships over time. Effective attitudes are observed in participants who appear to have a prevalence of positive feelings and views toward collaboration and who are consistently engaging in activities beyond defined roles and expectations.

Collaborators need to (a) share a common philosophy and goals and (b) be willing to be accountable for their own performance and for student progress in learning. In this setting, it is routine for colleagues to seek the wisdom, advice, and support of their colleagues. Teachers need to have "proactive attitudes" about initiating communication with their collaborative partners (Vargo, 1998). Learning to trust and respect each other, partners are less likely to be distracted by personal concerns and more likely to attend to the work at hand (Friend & Cook, 2000).

Team Process

The success of voluntary or mandated partnerships depends, to a great extent, on the processes that partners use to communicate and engage. The collaborative process, flexible enough to accommodate individual needs, can take place through formal and informal activities. It should incorporate ongoing organizational routines that fit the traits and demands of the environments and the people involved (Hunt, Doering, Hirose-Hatae, Maier, & Goetz, 2001; Kennedy, Higgins, & Pierce, 2002; Wolfe & Hall, 2003). Activities should be goal driven, and interactions seem to be most productive when teams focus on the collective agenda. Processes should be user friendly and allow participants to feel valued and engaged equally in decision making (Snell &

Figure 1. Elements of Collaboration

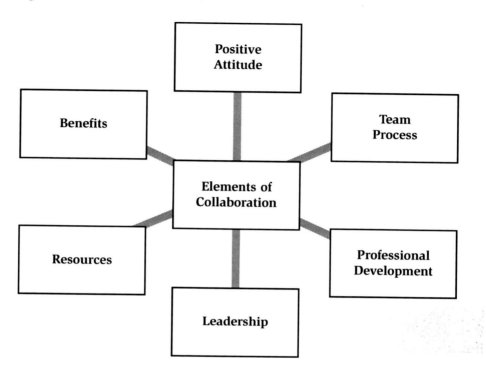

Janney, 2000). Although the process more or less regulates how things are done, teams need to allow sufficient flexibility to allow adjustments without causing major collisions in the system.

Professional Development

Both general and special educators need ongoing professional development, especially those who are faced with the demands of effectively working in an environment of inclusion. Whether it is through workshops, inservices, newsletters, online chat rooms, study groups, discussions, lectures, involvement in research projects, and graduate study, all teachers benefit from continuous professional development. Having the opportunity to visit other schools and classrooms can provide a rich experience for teachers who "show and share" their teaching strategies.

Whereas the focus of professional development activities may vary, leaders must clearly define the focus of the activities. Participants must perceive the professional development as valuable for the collaborative effort and as connected to classroom practice.

Professional development too often follows the "expert from outside" model, one that is imposed by administrators. This format seldom fosters interaction among the teachers or capitalizes on teachers' knowledge or expertise as professional educators. Giving teachers the opportunity to be teacher-leaders and co-planners of inservice events acknowledges teacher voice and allows them to participate in the crafting of a collaborative culture (Leonard, 2002; Zemelman, Daniels, & Hyde, 1993).

As teachers and administrators share expertise, strengths, and questions, they are likely to form collaborative partnerships throughout school activities. Because everyone learns differently and has individual interests, providing teachers with the opportunity to choose from a range of professional development possibilities can be helpful in motivating and energizing them. Professional development can enrich the lives of all professionals.

Leadership

Administrators at the district or school level, department chairs, area coordinators, or individual teachers can all initiate or provide leadership for collaborative partnerships. Leaders need to show a strong presence, one that is resourceful and proactive. Scheduling mutual planning time for teachers, identifying creative ways to use support staff (Hunt, Soto, Maier, & Doering, 2003), and monitoring student placement are tasks performed by school administrators that send a clear message of expectations to teachers attempting to collaborate.

Effective leadership results in increased participant self-concept, support for the work atmosphere, and encouragement to other members to enter into collaborative partnerships. Administrators need to give teachers the opportunity to be perceived as high-performing professionals. Volunteering or being appointed to leadership roles can be the impetus for professional growth and self-fulfilling rewards (Friend & Cook, 2000).

The school administrator, or other designated leaders, must support a school culture that celebrates collaboration and acknowledges those who lead and participate in the collaborative process. Ultimately, teachers should become leaders not because of public recognition but because of the intrinsic rewards of a job well done and the benefits gained for the children.

Resources

Different educational communities have varying needs, but we have found common resources that are basic to any collaborative effort (Fennick & Liddy, 2001; McLeskey & Waldron, 2002).

- Time is at the essence of collaborative efforts. Participants need to have time to plan and interact, as well as time to reflect and evaluate.
- Schools must have adequate financial support for collaboration, whether this support comes from the school budget or funding initiated through grant programs or external partnerships.

- Ongoing attention should be given to discussing and planning ways to improve resources. Whenever possible, teachers deserve additional compensation for successful collaborative efforts since it is part of their professional work (Leonard, 2002).

Benefits

Benefits of any change process must be experienced and evident. Participants need to discuss outcomes in concrete terms, not just as abstract constructs.

- Students with disabilities are exposed to an expanded curriculum, increased educational opportunities, an improved learning climate, and classroom instruction that is more engaging (Austin, 2001; Hunt et al., 2003).
- Teachers enhance their areas of expertise and learn from colleagues about how to implement pedagogical adjustments.
- One study also supported the notion that teachers stay in the profession longer when they experience success and feel supported (Barth, 1999).
- Collaboration creates a support system where even parents report having a greater opportunity to be a vital role in their children's education.

FRAMEWORK FOR EXAMINING A SCHOOL'S COLLABORATION EFFECTIVENESS

We have developed a framework for the assessment of collaborative efforts that uses a developmental perspective. The framework applies an "Elements of Collaboration Rubric" that identifies three distinct levels of development related to the elements of collaboration, as follows:

- Initial level.
- Emerging level.
- Effective level.

These levels are cross-matched to the elements essential to the success of teacher collaboration: positive attitude, team process, professional development, leadership, resources, and benefits (see Figure 2, "Elements of Collaboration; Rubric").

Using the rubric as a reference, team members record characteristics of a school's collaboration efforts in the appropriate place on a checklist (see Figure 3, "Elements of Collaboration: Checklist"). The checklist identifies the elements and the key indicators to consider as one examines a school's collaborative efforts and activities. The checklist also provides space to mark the level of performance and include anecdotal comments for further clarification.

Figure 2. Elements of Collaboration: Rubric

Element	Initial Level	Emerging Level	Effective Level
Positive Attitude	Mixed Feelings/views: (some positive, some negative)	More positive feelings (comfortable, included, supportive, trusting)	Prevalence of positive feelings/views toward collaboration
	Establishing commitment/ motivation	Increasing signs of commitment/motivation	Consistent engagement in activities beyond prescribed role and expectations
	Defining roles	Clearer understanding of collaborative roles	Embraces and expands roles
	Determining accountability	Willingness to be accountable	Sets high standards of performance
	Defining philosophy, goals, expertise	Shared philosophy/goals Appreciation of colleagues' expertise and contributions	Ongoing reflection about philosophy/goals/practice
			Reaches out to colleagues for advice/support/expertise
Team Process	Communication avenues identified	Adequate opportunity to communicate	Active communication between colleagues (frequent, productive, flexible, and sensitive)
		Interactions involve a sense of "give and take"	
	Developing initial formal processes (routines, roles, expectations, meetings)	Reasonable and clear formal processes implemented (routines, expectations, meetings)	Activities—goal driven, user friendly, and respects participants' values and decisions
	Defining team roles	Interactions focus collective effort rather than individual "wants"	Processes honored and adapted to meet changing needs
Professional Development	Determining focus	Gaining clarity of focus	Clear focus which incorporates standards, expectations, and values
	Beginning to express teacher voice in development plans	Teachers have a clear voice in plans	Teachers/administrators collaboratively plan and lead
	Determining connection between development activities and classroom practice	More evident connection between activities and classroom	Content transfers to class or other collaborative efforts
	Identifying involvement of in-house expertise and talent	Teachers and administrators share expertise	Professional Development supports best practice which leads to public sharing (conferences, publications)
	Developing a plan/schedule for professional development activities	Ongoing activities, flexibly scheduled with options	Ongoing, flexible, multiple options
	Addresses participant groups separately	Emerging community building climate	Community building climate

continues

Figure 2. *Continued*

Element	Initial Level	Emerging Level	Effective Level
Leadership	Identifying leadership opportunities and roles	Shared leadership roles	Strong presence of leader(s)
	Designing supportive climate	Supportive climate felt by most participants	Supportive climate
	Determining initiatives to motivate participation or lead roles	Proactive encouragement for leadership roles and decision making	Participants volunteer for leadership roles
	Designing ways to recognize collaboration effort	Effort is recognized Accountability system is clear	Participants hold themselves to high expectations. Participation is self-fulfilling rather than for public recognition
Resources	Targeting needs (finances, staff, time, support systems, scheduling, supplies, space)	Adequately targets needs	Targets needs, provides to the maximum extent possible and conducts ongoing assessment: Participants initiate funding and resource opportunities (grants, partnerships)
Benefits	Defining benefits	Some benefits of collaboration evident	Benefits continue to be evident
	Creating opportunities for participants to experience benefits	Less abstraction, more experience	Benefits lived and prominent
	Planning ways to publicize benefits for education and acknowledgement	Efforts made to publicize and recognize efforts and benefits	Publicity and recognition of efforts and benefits are shared responsibility of several constituents

A completed checklist for a particular school can help identify the developmental level of each of the elements and can provide an overall, big picture assessment of progress toward effective collaboration. A sample checklist on a fictitious school shows what a completed checklist might look like and what generalizations one might draw (see Figure 4, "Elements of Collaboration: Checklist Sample").

Complete the checklist, determining the level of development for the school. Rate and make comments on each of the elements and their indicators. Use the rubric for further clarification of levels (for a sample school's checklist summary, see box).

Figure 3. Elements of Collaboration: Checklist

Element	Initial	Emerging	Effective	Comments
Positive Attitude				
Feelings and views toward collaboration				
Commitment and motivation				
Roles: clarity, understanding and acceptance				
Accountability: for teacher and student performance				
Philosophy, goals, and expertise				
Team Process				
Communication and work relationships				
Processes: routines, roles, expectations, meetings				
Team roles				
Professional Development				
Focus				
Teacher voice				
Connection with classroom practice				
Use of in-house expertise and talent				
Scheduling and delivery options				
Sense of community				
Leadership				
Leader(s)				
Work climate				
Teacher leadership and decision making				
Accountability/motivation to lead				
Resources				
Targets needs (time, people, finances, scheduling, supplies, space, and other)				
Benefits				
Identified and evident				
Lived vs. abstract				
Effort is publicly acknowledged				

ELEMENTS OF COLLABORATION: ACTION PLAN

The final step in the framework is the completion of an action plan, which precisely targets future efforts to support collaboration for those elements at the lower levels of development (see Figure 5, "Action Plan: Elements of Collaboration").

Figure 4. Elements of Collaboration: Checklist Sample

Element	Initial	Emerging	Effective	Comments and Key
				I = Interviews **O = Observations**
Positive Attitude				
Feelings and views toward collaboration			X	I—Positive about collaboration, co-teaching.
Commitment and motivation			X	O—Twelve co-teaching teams.
Roles: clarity, understanding, and acceptance			X	I—Compliments for each other. O/I—High standards.
Accountability—for teacher and student performance			X	I—Welcomed each others expertise/advice. Desire to learn from one
Philosophy, goals, and expertise			X	another.
Team Process				
Communication and work relationships		X		I—Generally satisfied, although some co-teaching relationships more
Processes: routines, roles, expectations, and meetings		X		productive than others. Some teams more experienced.
Team Roles			X	Clarity in roles improving. More formal processes needed. Climate fosters professional relationships, teams across the school. O—Co-teaching teams function well.
Professional Development				
Focus			X	O/I—Focus prevailed through
Teacher voice		X		professional development (PD) activities.
Connection with classroom practice			X	I—Teachers involved in planning
Use of in-house expertise and talent			X	(most spec ed teachers).
Scheduling and delivery options		X		O—Evidence of PD applications in
Sense of community			X	classes. I—Use of both general and special educators' expertise. I—Community building in PD activities.
Leadership				
Leader(s)			X	I—Model keeps changing to meet
Work climate			X	students' needs. Teachers indicate supportive work
Teacher leadership and decision making		X		environment. New administrator hired to help with instructional lead-
Accountability/motivation to lead			X	ership. Special educators—strong leaders. Teacher leaders across school. High expectations for students and teachers. Teachers appear proud of their accomplishments.
Resources				
Targets needs (time, people, finances, scheduling, supplies, space, other)		X		I—Improving, time better used. Never enough help.
Benefits				
Identified and Evident			X	O—Students with disabilities not easily identified in classes.
Lived vs. abstract		X		I—Teachers report benefits in
Effort is publicly acknowledged		X		student learning and teacher performance.

Figure 5. Action Plan: Elements of Collaboration

Element	What Needs Improvement?	Task?	Who Is Responsible?	Completion Date?
Positive Attitudes				
Team Process				
Professional Development				
Leadership				
Resources				
Benefits				

At this point in the framework, school personnel must be fully involved in decisions. This is the perfect opportunity to empower the faculty and staff, hearing and blending their voices, providing opportunity for leadership, and recognizing the vested interests of faculty and staff in the entire process.

The logistics of completing the action plan are fairly straightforward. The information that is recorded in the checklist provides data to decision makers who will attempt to prioritize needs. This decision making must be a shared process among all collaborative partners.

The action plan articulates in writing the activities to be accomplished, the persons responsible for them, and deadlines for achievement. The plan becomes a roadmap toward improvement of school collaboration.

FINAL THOUGHTS

In the framework for collaboration, a rubric, checklist, and an action plan serve as practical tools for educators—both administrators and teachers—to

Sample Collaboration: Using the Rubric and Checklist

Working in an urban public school with special and general educators to improve school collaboration, the consultant was hearing numerous concerns expressed by the teachers and the principal, as follows:

- What does collaboration look like in classroom teaching and planning?

- When do we find the time to collaborate?

- How do we share beliefs and routines with our co-teachers?

- Can teachers have input in the design of professional development?

- Who is responsible for leading us and keeping us all accountable for our roles and responsibilities?

- How do we get resources?

- What are the benefits of collaboration?

Over a period of 2 years, the consultant examined collaboration in this school. Interviews with the school administration, observations of classroom instruction, and one-on-one interviews with classroom and special education teachers helped the consultant and school personnel begin to clarify specific needs and challenges.

Efficient Data Collection

At the beginning of this process, it became clear team members needed a systematic way to collect and record information. Having a structured framework also would ensure that all elements of collaboration were included in the data collection. Thus, the consultant used a rubric as a guide to identifying the developmental levels of the elements of collaboration seen in this school. To record this information, team members used a checklist matching the information on the rubric.

Effective Diagnostic Information

The sample completed checklist reflects a big picture, yet at the same time, a diagnostic view of the collaboration efforts at this fictitious school. The reader can see that the recorder has noted when information was gleaned from either observation or interviews with individuals in the school. Looking at the checklist and viewing where the school performs developmentally according to the elements, a picture emerges which will help the school in future planning.

Indicators and Action Plans

On a very positive note for this school, no element indicators are found at the "Initial" level; and the majority of the indicators appear at the "Emerging" and "Effective" levels. The element of Positive Attitude seems to be at the "Effective" level, as do Leadership and Professional Development elements. Team Process is emerging. Routines are becoming habits, and processes are being reconfigured to meet the needs of students and teachers.

For the Leadership element, one indicator may need focus: The school needs to continue to find ways to motivate teacher leadership and decision making. Also, school leaders must create more opportunities to encourage teacher voice and find more options for delivering professional development. Indicators in Team Process, Professional Development, Resources, and Benefits are at the emerging level and may require ongoing monitoring and evaluation.

guide and help a school prioritize tasks to achieve success in collaborative practices with special and general educators. The framework provides a user-friendly way to organize information about a collaborative process.

REFERENCES

Austin, V. (2001). Teachers' beliefs about co-teaching. *Remedial and Special Educators, 22,* 4.

Barth, R. S. (1999). *The teacher leader.* Providence: The Rhode Island Foundation.

Fennick, E., & Liddy, D. (2001). Responsibilities and preparation for collaborative teaching: Co-teachers' perspectives. *Teacher Education and Special Education, 24,* 229–240.

Friend, M., & Cook, L. (2000). *Interactions: Collaboration skills for school professionals* (3rd ed.). New York: Longman.

Hunt, P., Doering, K., Hirose-Hatae, A., Maier, J., & Goetz, L. (2001). Across-program collaboration to support students with and without disabilities in a general education classroom. *The Journal of the Association for Persons with Severe Handicaps, 26,* 240–256.

Hunt, P., Soto, G., Maier, J., & Doering, K. (2003). Collaborative teaming to support students at risk and students with severe disabilities in general education classrooms. *Exceptional Children, 69,* 315–332.

Kennedy, K., Higgins, K., & Pierce, T. (2002). Collaborative partnerships among teachers of students who are gifted and have learning disabilities. *Intervention in School and Clinic, 38,* 36–49.

Leonard, L. (2002). Schools as professional communities: Addressing the collaborative change. *International Electronic Journal of Leadership in Learning, 6*(17). Retrieved September 2004 from http:// www.ucalgary.ca/ ~ iejll/

McLeskey, J., & Waldron, N. L. (2002). Inclusion and school change: Teacher perceptions regarding curricular and instructional adaptations. *Teacher Education and Special Education, 25,* 41–54.

Schmitz, C. D., Baber, S. J., John, D. M., & Brown, K. S. (2000). Creating the 21st century school of education: Collaboration, community, and partnership in St. Louis. *Peabody Journal of Education, 75,* 64–85.

Snell, M. E., & Janney, R. (2000). *Teachers' guides to inclusive practices: Collaborative teaming.* Baltimore: Paul H. Brookes.

Vargo, S. (1998). Consulting teacher-to-teacher. *TEACHING Exceptional Children, 30*(3), 54–55.

Walther-Thomas, C., Korinek, L., McLaughlin, V. L., & Williams, B. T. (2002). *Collaboration for inclusive education: Developing successful programs.* Boston: Allyn & Bacon.

Wolfe, P. S., & Hall, T. E. (2003). Making inclusion a reality for students with severe disabilities. *TEACHING Exceptional Children, 35*(4), 56–60.

Zemelman, S., Daniels, H., & Hyde, A. (1993). *Best practice: New standards for teaching and learning in America's schools.* Portsmouth, NH: Heinemann.

Originally published in *TEACHING Exceptional Children,* Vol. 38, No. 5, pp. 49–56.

10

New Teacher Teams to Support Integrated Comprehensive Services

Elise M. Frattura and Colleen A. Capper

Most educators agree that students with disabilities should spend as much time as possible in the general education classroom. However, this expectation frustrates many educators because they do not receive support in ways that ensure the success of students. This article describes an integrated comprehensive service (ICS) delivery model that uses four teams to provide educator support for the benefit of all students in general education.

Our extensive research and practice with an ICS delivery model over the past 12 years—in 10 different schools, at the elementary, middle, and high school levels and located in rural, suburban, and urban districts—indicates that educators need to rethink the team structures in their schools to implement and sustain ICS (see box, "What Is an Integrated Comprehensive Service Delivery Model?"). These new team structures are necessary because research suggests that sustaining inclusive practices over time is difficult. For example, in their 4-year-long study of a middle school, Sindelar, Shearer, Yendol-Hoppey, and Liebert (2006) focused on the sustainability of inclusive education. The study indicated that changes in leadership, teacher turnover, and changes in state and district assessment policies resulted in failure to sustain inclusion. Those changes, in turn, led to a reduction of resources and philosophical commitment to inclusion.

Our research and practice suggests that sustaining ICS is possible when teachers are full participants in school decisions through membership in four specific teams. Three of these teams are at the school level: a planning team,

What Is an Integrated Comprehensive Service Delivery Model?

An integrated comprehensive service (ICS) delivery model is a model that organizes professional staff by the needs of each learner instead of clustering learners by label (Frattura & Capper, in press). An ICS model does not assign staff members to a unit or program and place them in separate classrooms. Instead, support staff and general education teachers work collaboratively to bring appropriate instructional supports to each child in integrated school and community environments. This model thereby establishes an integrated home base in support of belonging for all learners (Frattura & Capper).

The word *integrated* refers to the environments that all students, regardless of need or legislative eligibility, access throughout their day in school and nonschool settings. That is, in integrated environments, students with a variety of needs and gifts learn together in both small and large groupings that are flexible in nature. A school that uses an ICS delivery model has no spaces that are designated only for those students with disabilities.

The term *comprehensive* refers to the array of services and supports, in addition to a differentiated curriculum and instruction, that accommodate the various learning needs of children to ensure their success in school. ICS results in the sharing of resources and choreographed services on the basis of the needs, strengths, and interests of each learner.

a service delivery team, and a grade-level design team; the fourth team, the districtwide service delivery team, functions at the district level. These teams engage in

- Shared decision making, that is, providing opportunities that allow individuals in the school community to be involved in implementation decisions.

- Staff design, that is, strategically assigning teachers and staff to students and classes in ways that build teacher capacity and maximize student learning.

- Student support, that is, strategically assigning students to classes in ways that do not segregate them, that maximize students' opportunities to learn in heterogeneous groups, and that create the conditions for optimal student learning.

Educators frequently focus on instruction and curriculum and assume that they do not have control over structure, policy, or procedures. The work of these four teams disrupts this assumption. In this article, we first briefly describe each team. Then, in the following sections, for each team, we delineate team goals, team membership, steps that the team can take to implement ICS, and ways to evaluate their efforts.

THE TEAMS

Overview

In schools with shared leadership, a schoolwide team—often known as a school learning team, site council, school planning team, shared decision-making team, or educational planning committee—frequently functions as an oversight committee for many school decisions. In this article, we use the term *school planning team*. In a school with shared decision making, such a team must be one of the essential teams that deals with the entire school. The school planning team is primarily responsible for collecting student-performance data and school-specific data, as well as setting annual or long-term goals for school improvement.

The second key decision-making team for initiating and implementing ICS is the school's service delivery team. This team functions as an offshoot of the school planning team specifically to analyze and redesign the way that services are offered. The service delivery team is also responsible for identifying the necessary changes in school and district-based policy and procedures for implementing ICS.

The third type of key decision-making team consists of grade-level design teams. These teams include teams of teachers at each grade level who are responsible for setting up the specific staff design for each grade level, as well as the instructional and curricular services for that grade level.

The districtwide service delivery team represents the fourth key decision-making team. This team's primary function is to ensure that service delivery is consistent across the district. The team's primary responsibility is to share information from the individual school teams to develop consistency and fluidity across the district for all students. For example, the team may want to confirm that a child moving from fifth to sixth grade is able to maintain services that are similar to those in the fifth grade and are based on his or her individualized service plan (ISP) or individualized education program (IEP). This team is the glue that holds the service delivery model together in Grades K–12.

A primary consideration for all four teams is team membership. The teams must represent a broad range of individuals who typically support students who struggle in the school. Such individuals might include the English language learners [ELL] teacher, an at-risk teacher, Title I staff, and special education teachers. In addition, team membership should ensure that teams consist of individuals who are demographically representative of the proportion of culturally and linguistically diverse people in the school and district. That is, all the teams should include the same proportion of students of a specific minority group as the proportion of members of that minority group in the school and in the district. Obviously, for example, if only 1% of the students are culturally and linguistically diverse, then 1% of the committee membership should be culturally and linguistically diverse. When teams—for example, the school planning team—include community members or families, these community members and families should represent the cultural, linguistic, and income diversity of the school and district. To encourage families or community members to participate, schools should consider providing transportation, child care, and language interpreters if needed (Lopez, 2003).

All four of these teams must set ground rules for discussion and decisions. In addition, the teams must all decide in what ways and how frequently they will communicate the progress of the team with the other three teams and with other school personnel. Further, the teams must decide how they will receive specific feedback from the other three teams and from other school personnel about their work.

School Planning Team

As previously mentioned, the school planning team is responsible for collecting and analyzing student data, as well as school-specific data. Frattura and Capper (in press) suggests a set of questions that can guide the evaluation of services for students. The school planning team can facilitate this evaluation. Team membership must include representatives from all stakeholders of the school community, including the school administrator, teachers, parents, students, other staff, and community members. A school planning team typically does the following (Conzemius & O'Neil, 2001):

- Focuses on student learning at the site.
- Serves as a forum for diverse perspectives from the school, home, and community to ensure the exchange of a variety of viewpoints.
- Provides participatory shared decision making at each site to create the individual school's structure and culture (within the district mission).
- Promotes communication among parents, community members, professional and support personnel, students, and administrators.

The school planning team can be responsible for curricular, instructional, and personnel budgets and can then make difficult decisions in support of the school and district mission. Often, a school planning team analyzes students' scores, discusses areas of concern and resolution, and then creates comprehensive school goals.

While the school planning team is addressing the goals on the basis of the data analysis, it can define and evaluate progress. The other three teams will also have their own goals and evaluation strategies that they will share with the school planning team.

School Service Delivery Team

The school service delivery team consists of teachers and administrators whose primary focus is to assess how services are being offered to and for all learners. The primary responsibility of the school service delivery team is to assess the quality of ICS on an ongoing basis, with emphasis on equity, structure of services, access to high-quality teaching and learning, and development of appropriate funding mechanisms and policies (Frattura & Capper, in press).

Services and programs provided within the school form the basis for membership on the school service delivery team. The team needs a representative from each unit, grade level, department, or academy to give voice to all stakeholders and to represent all children in the school. In addition, teachers representing the different programs offered in the school (e.g., ELL, Title I, at risk) should constitute the remainder of the teacher leaders on the committee. As many studies confirm, the participation of the school administrator is essential to the operations of the team (Fullan, 1999). The school administrator should be an equal member of the team, with little or no veto power but with the opportunity to use his or her skills of persuasion. In many schools that have functioning school service delivery teams, the districtwide administrator for student services and special education and the director of curriculum and instruction may participate as equal members of the team. These individuals often have the ability to obtain and reallocate resources to assist in the movement from programs to services; for example, they can facilitate the commingling of funds in support of all learners. The school service delivery team should not have more than 10 to 12 members, primarily so that all members can participate in decisions. Individuals on the team should have strong opinions about educational services for all learners.

The goals of the school service delivery team are simple:

- To better meet the needs of each learner in a comprehensive manner in integrated school and community environments.

- To take a clear look at the structural barriers to providing the most comprehensive integrated services possible and to reconstruct a model of service delivery that will provide students with minimal fragmentation within the school day.

- To attend to any symbolic and procedural practices that perpetuate the division between the haves and the have-nots, for example, field trips, school ceremonies, and banquets.

Seven specific steps and processes help this team achieve its goals:

1. The team must have the opportunity to discuss what integrated comprehensive services are and what they are not. They may want to share readings about ideas related to ICS (see Peterson & Hittie, 2003, for a comprehensive list of research in support of ICS). The team can then reflect and think about what it means to move toward ICS for all learners and decide by consensus what moving toward ICS could mean.

2. All team members must agree about the importance of adopting a philosophy of ICS. Many school teams make decisions concerning the core principles of ICS without reaching a consensus. Unless teams

make such decisions by consensus, they default to a traditional structure of programs and compliance-driven policy that undermines growth and education for students who require additional services. The team should not force change. If team members cannot generate enough interest in ICS at the school, they should continue to ask such questions as the following:

- Why do the children who have the least ability to generalize have the most fragmented schedules?
- Could we do more for all learners if we worked together instead of in our own separate silos?
- When we say all learners, do we really mean *all*?

3. The team next draws a picture describing how the school currently meets the needs of children who are challenged—or the needs of children who challenge how we teach. That is, they draw a picture of the school's current program delivery model. This picture should address the question: What programs are currently in place for students who struggle in our school? The picture of this current delivery model must be as detailed as possible.

4. The team uses the information developed in the preceding steps to conduct a gap analysis. The team compares the current service delivery model with the principles of ICS and evidenced-based practices. The team can then determine the locations of any gaps between what ICS entails and what is currently happening with the service delivery picture in the school.

5. Participants then list current practices in their school that focus on prevention and determine whether these practices are comprehensive, integrated, and effective enough to build success for every learner. If these practices align with the ICS principles, then the school should continue these practices in the new service delivery model.

6. The team members brainstorm their vision and hopes for service delivery in their school, basing these visions and hopes on the principles of ICS. Team members then draw a picture of the future service delivery model on large paper. They list this vision and these hopes without considering any budgetary concerns, since such concerns can limit recommendations. Although every district has budget limitations, administrators and facilitators are often able to creatively address financial concerns to support an ICS model by commingling funds or by reallocating them. Limiting the model by using a financial formula can also limit recommendations. Often staff members find that drawing the picture of the new model is difficult and instead use a table or diagram to outline it.

7. The school service delivery team then moves on to the final step, which is to develop a plan for achieving the new service delivery

model. At this point, the decision making needs to move to the grade-level design teams that will be responsible for turning the vision into reality.

The school service delivery team meets as often as necessary at the beginning of the change process but may reduce its meeting schedule when the grade-level design teams begin their work. The school service delivery team is then primarily responsible for evaluation activities and may reconvene to discuss feedback or major concerns regarding the efficacy of the model. In so doing, the members of the school service delivery team should examine what is working and what is not and determine options for creative solutions without reverting back to an old model of segregating children. To prevent the marginalization of any child, all educators have a responsibility to educate the next generation of children together—structurally, symbolically, and academically. Therefore, the pendulum must not swing back to segregation. Nonetheless, we cannot discount the possibility of strife in the process. Change is difficult, and there will be times when teachers and administrators need support from the school service delivery team members.

Grade-Level Design Teams

As previously discussed, most school service delivery teams provide recommendations that result in a grade-based model of service delivery. For example, one team of teachers and staff may work with a range of learners at 8th grade and other teams may work with a range of learners at 10th and 11th grade. If grade level is the primary basis for school structure, structuring the support model by grades makes sense. If the school uses a structure that consists of small learning academies, then providing services that are based on the academy structure makes more sense. Either way, it is not logical to continue a model by specialization (ED, LD, at risk, ELL, Title I, etc.) in a school that uses a structure by grades, houses, academies, or some other configuration. Educators should therefore avoid configuring support in a manner that makes particular teachers responsible for groups of labeled students across grades; that is, the school should not configure support so that one teacher is responsible for all students with the ED label across three, four, or more grades. That practice disconnects teacher specializations and the graded structures of schools and results in fragmentation and failure-based programs.

A primary responsibility of the grade-level design teams is to assign students and staff in ways that support ICS principles. The school planning team completes the ICS analysis; but the school service delivery and grade-level design teams develop, implement, and evaluate the service delivery design. These latter two teams are the ones that bring the vision to life. The school service delivery team suggests to the grade-level design teams possible ways of supporting students. The grade-level design teams are responsible for the actual implementation. These grade-level design teams make big schools small, make large numbers of students individuals, and minimize such bureaucratic measures as programming students en masse or clustering students by label or by statutory regulations.

The grade-level design teams should include all individuals who are assigned to a specific grade level or have volunteered at that level to provide service to students with disabilities, students who speak English as a second language, students who are deemed at risk of failing to complete school, and other students. Each grade-level design team must include the general educators, special educators, at-risk teachers, ELL teachers, and other teachers assigned to the grade-level team by the process that the school service delivery team has completed. In addition, school social workers, guidance counselors, the school psychologist, teachers of gifted and talented students, speech and language pathologists, and other support may focus on particular grade levels for a variety of reasons. For example, guidance counselors may become part of a grade-level design team and provide service only to students at that particular grade level, or a speech and language clinician might be assigned to a kindergarten–first grade cluster, since the language needs are high in those two grades. The grade-level design team specifies the role of these personnel, but the role should include direct support to students in heterogeneous groups. Finally, a representative of the school service delivery team should serve on each grade-level design team as a liaison between the two teams.

The goals of the grade-level design teams are to meet the individual needs of each learner, from children with mild learning disabilities or third-year ELL students to students with severe and profound cognitive disabilities or extreme behavioral challenges caused by mental illness, as well as children with average or above-average abilities and skills. These teams therefore strategically assign staff to courses and classrooms and place students to ensure that students are not segregated and to maximize student learning.

The grade-level design teams have three additional functions. First, they must determine the professional development that is necessary to build the ability of teachers to teach a range of learners in their classrooms. Second, they must help staff include planning time in their work days and weeks so that staff members can collaborate to meet student needs. Third, they must help secure the resources to carry out these first two functions. A representative of each grade-level design team then takes the professional development, planning time, and resource needs to the school service delivery team, which can then coordinate professional development and planning time, as well as obtain resources for these needs in collaboration with the school planning team.

The grade-level design teams use 10 processes and steps:

1. The school service delivery team first determines the membership on each grade-level design team. For example, if all first-grade teachers in a school comprise the first-grade-level design team, then the school service delivery team may suggest assigning a special education teacher and a

bilingual specialist to serve all first-grade students. As the planning process continues, team membership may change, depending on the configuration of the new service delivery.

2. The grade-level design team lists the students within that particular grade level who struggle. This list includes students eligible for special education, Title I students, at-risk students, ELLs, and other students who are struggling but have not met eligibility criteria for a program.

3. Each of the students who is eligible for special education must have an IEP. To assist the team in determining needs and calculating the optimal amount of individual, small-group, and large-group support, the grade-level design team should create an ISP for each of the struggling students who is not eligible for special education.

4. The grade-level design team then strategically assigns students to particular classes or courses. Grade-level team members often divide the group of students into smaller caseloads to enable each staff person to better determine specific needs. Most teams attempt to place students with teachers whose expertise matches the students' needs or to place students with a staff member who is familiar with the student and is willing to continue with that student, as long as students are naturally placed into integrated classrooms and caseloads are balanced (see box, "Student Placement in Classrooms"). For example, placing all students with high behavioral needs in the caseload of one teacher is not logical, because the teacher will never be able to proactively support 10 or more students with significant high needs in two or three different classrooms. However, placing 1 or 2 students with high behavioral needs on the caseload of a teacher with 8 other students who do not have such needs is logical.

5. After determining the primary areas of need and the necessary support, the team determines the schedule for each student, on the basis of the typical learner's schedule at that grade level. For each student's schedule, the team identifies areas where the student is receiving individual, small-group, or large-group instruction with or without support. Students with the greatest needs often have the most transitions. Therefore, to prevent later problems and to allow students to begin their year with a schedule that is likely to remain unchanged, educators at the middle school and high school levels should hand-schedule students with specific needs before they begin the mass scheduling by grade level and subjects.

6. After developing a schedule for each student, the team drafts a teacher schedule to determine when and where teachers need to provide appropriate support. Where conflicts occur, the team members decide how they can work together to support and resolve the conflicts.

7. After support staff members have identified their caseloads and outlined schedules for students and staff, the real work begins. Support teachers and general educators need to determine exactly how their work together will look, including determining when they will team teach, when the

Student Placement in Classrooms

The concept of natural proportions should guide all decisions about student placement in classrooms. For example, if 12% of the students in a school have special needs, then no more than 12% of the students in a single classroom should have special needs. If English language learners (ELLs) comprise 10% of the school population, then the proportion of ELLs in any single classroom or course should be no more than 10%. Educators should balance the percentage of students with special needs across classrooms, in the same proportion as in that grade.

In addition, a continuum of support should guide student placement decisions. That is, not all students who require support need direct support from a specialist. Some students need the support of a team-taught classroom where a general education teacher and a support teacher (e.g., a special education teacher or a bilingual teacher) teach the course together. The goal of such a teaching arrangement should be to build the teaching capacity of the general teacher so that team-teaching support is not necessary. Some students may require direct instruction from a support teacher for part of the school day in the general education classroom. Others may benefit from the support of a teaching assistant or school volunteer for part of the school day. Still other students may only require a support teacher to check in with the general education teacher on a regular basis for feedback and assistance or for on-call support. Some students can receive high-quality support from their peers in collaborative learning classrooms. Educators should not place students in particular classrooms with the assumption that they all need direct support from a specialist; the primary purpose of support teachers is to build the capacity of general educators to teach to a range of student needs in their classrooms. Also, the school should not place students in different classrooms at a grade level in a manner that does not allow them to receive the support that they may need.

support teacher will be in the room for support only, and when the support teacher will assist with flexible groupings. After organizing the teaming schedule, support teachers and general educators need to develop the curriculum and assessment for each section of the day.

8. Each grade-level design team should meet at least weekly to evaluate its efforts, including determining how the support is working and discussing where more support may be necessary. Teams at one grade level may need to meet with teams at other grade levels if they cannot work out the necessary small-group or individual support within their grade level. Such meetings can help give students full support across their grade levels (horizontally) and throughout all the grades (vertically).

9. If the school service delivery team has recommended that grade-level design teams follow their students to the next grade and return to their original grade in the third year (called *looping*), then teams should begin planning for the next school year in February by using the steps outlined

in the preceding paragraphs and by using feedback obtained from data analysis.

10. Grade-level design teams frequently collect student achievement data as a prime determinant of their success. They also work with the school service delivery team to obtain feedback that shows how parents, students, and staff experience the evolving changes of the service delivery structure for all learners. In addition, they update the school service delivery team on their progress and any concerns that they should take to the school planning team.

Districtwide Service Delivery Team

Students may receive services in an elementary school that meets their individual needs (such as time in the day for sensory integration or inclusion with peers for most of the day). However, when these students advance to the next grade level or school, their ISP or IEP may change because the staff has designed a model that cannot meet those individual needs. Educators at every school must be responsible for developing a service delivery model that meets the needs of every possible student. When implementing ICS, districts should therefore institute a districtwide service delivery team to work through issues that may affect the district as a whole.

The districtwide service delivery team should include a representative from each school service delivery team throughout the district. In addition, the district director of special education or student services and the district director of instruction should also be team members.

The goal of the districtwide service delivery team is to "take care of the whole." That is, the districtwide team is responsible for clarifying differences across school service delivery teams and working toward developing a continuous model for kindergarten through 12th grade throughout the district. Students then do not need to fit into different models that each individual school develops.

Districtwide service delivery teams typically meet four times each year. After the team clarifies areas of need or concern, the team sets its agenda and moves forward. At times, the team may ask staff or administrators to join it so that the team can obtain more detailed information regarding a specific concern. An example might be determining how an elementary school uses a sensory room and how such a room might work at the middle school level.

The districtwide service delivery team monitors the status of service delivery at each school. The members of the school service delivery team on the districtwide committee use the ICS evaluations to assess their progress toward ICS.

FINAL THOUGHTS

If ICS is to become a reality in schools, educators need to be deliberate about decision making and team structures. ICS moves far beyond typical team structures in schools; it can use general education–based grade-level teams, department teams, or strategic planning teams. In addition, team structures that support ICS also move beyond typical special education teams. Such structures can use prereferral intervention teams and special education evaluation teams. The simple structure and function of the three school-based teams and the district-level service delivery team described in this article can transform how decisions are made, who is involved in the decisions, how the school uses its resources, how it assigns teachers, and how it serves students. This transformation can move far beyond compliance—it can result in a high-quality education for every student in the school.

REFERENCES

Conzemius, A., & O'Neil, J. (2001). *Building shared responsibility for student learning*. Alexandria, VA: Association for Supervision and Curriculum Development.

Frattura, E., & Capper, C. (in press). *Leading for social justice: Transforming schools for all learners*. Thousand Oaks, CA: Corwin Press.

Fullan, M. (1999). *Change forces: The sequel*. Philadelphia: Falmer.

Lopez, G. R. (2003). The value of hard work: Lessons on parent involvement from an (im)migrant household. *Harvard Educational Review, 71*, 416–437.

Peterson, M., & Hittie, M. M. (2003). *Inclusive teaching: Creating effective schools for all learners*. San Francisco: Allyn & Bacon.

Sindelar, P., Shearer, D., Yendol-Hoppey, D., & Liebert, T. (2006). The sustainability of inclusive school reform. *Exceptional Children, 72*, 317–331.

Originally published in *TEACHING Exceptional Children*, Vol. 39, No. 4, pp. 16–21.